Memorable Moments...

Selected Sermons
Of
Evangelist and Co-Pastor
Susie C. Owens

Compiled by Beverly Lucas
Edited by Sherry Hubbard

All Scripture quotations are taken from the *Authorized King James Version* of the Bible unless otherwise noted.

Memorable Moments
Copyright © 2003 by Co-Pastor Susie C. Owens
610 Rhode Island Ave., N.E.
Washington, D.C., 20005
Phone: (202) 529-4547

ISBN 1-890146-07-2

Printed in the United States of America

Graphic design by Mark Burrier of Octavo Designs

CONTENTS

ACKNOWLEDGMENTS

Special thanks to: Mrs. Serita Jakes of The Potters House, and Co-Pastor Jo Ann Browning of Ebenezer Methodist Church for their endorsements and loving support.

Also, I would like to express my sincere thanks to all those who helped make this book a reality:

To Beverly Lucas, who served as the compiler, production manager and coordinator.

To Sherry Hubbard, who edited all the material.

To Ludie Simay, who selected the tapes.

To Patricia Little of PNL Designs.

ABOUT THE AUTHOR

EVANGELIST SUSIE C. OWENS is a native Bostonian and a product of the Boston Public School System. She is a graduate of Bethel Bible Institute, where she earned an Associate of Arts degree in New Testament Studies in 1970. Understanding her call to teach, she pursued the field of education, graduating from Brooks College in 1972 with a Bachelor of Arts degree in Early Childhood Education. In May of 1999, she received a Master of Arts degree in Religious Studies from Howard University School of Divinity.

She has been in the ministry for over twenty-five years during which time she has traveled extensively throughout the United States as well as abroad. Her unique presentation of the gospel has enabled her to minister to many denominations and organizations and as a result she is a much sought after lecturer, teacher, leader, and counselor. Moreover her gift has made room for her, allowing her to minister on national platforms to tens of thousands. It has been her privilege to serve at various women's retreats, marriage seminar, youth rallies and crusades. God has granted her favor in the secular arena where she has had the honor of serving as Secretary for the Mayor's office of Religious Affairs in the District of Columbia.

She has received numerous awards and citations, most noteworthy among them, the distinct honor of Mother of the Year for the District of Columbia, an honor bestowed upon her by the American Mothers Association - an interracial, ecumenical organization - for her outstanding work in the field of parenting.

She is the wife of Bishop Alfred A. Owens, Jr., D. Min., pastor of Greater Mt. Calvary Holy Church in Washington, D.C., and Vice Bishop of the Mt Calvary Holy Churches of America, Inc. Evangelist Owens serves alongside her husband in ministry as the Co-Pastor of Greater Mt. Calvary Holy Church, a progressive, inner-city church with an adult membership of more than 6,000. She serves as Instructor of the Calvary Bible Institute with more than nine hundred students. She is also the coordinator of the Greater Mt. Calvary Holy Church's Annual Women's Conference. She is the author of Unless Two Agree which is a book dedicated to "team ministry" and shares a weekly television broadcast with her husband. Evangelist Owens serves as a member of the Evangelistic Board and the Trustee Board. In her spare time, she enjoys the theater and reading. Finally, she is the proud mother of two children, Alfred Thomas and Kr:istel Moneek and grandmother of three, Darian Isaiah, Nicholas Thomas and William Isaac.

A Touch to Live

And when Jesus was passed over again by ship unto the other side, much people gathered unto him: and he was nigh unto the sea.

22   And, behold, there cometh one of the rulers of the synagogue, Jairus by name; and when he saw him, he fell at his feet,

23   And besought him greatly, saying, My little daughter lieth at the point of death: I pray thee, come and lay thy hands on her, that she may be healed; and she shall live.

24   And Jesus went with him; and much people followed him, and thronged him.

25   And a certain woman, which had an issue of blood twelve years,

26   And had suffered many things of many physicians, and had spent all that she had, and was nothing bettered, but rather grew worse,

27   When she had heard of Jesus, came in the press behind, and touched his garment.

28   For she said, If I may touch but his clothes, I shall be whole.

29   And straightway the fountain of her blood was dried up; and she felt in her body that she was healed of that plague.

30   And Jesus, immediately knowing in himself that virtue had gone out of him, turned him about in the press, and said, Who touched my clothes?

31   And his disciples said unto him, Thou seest the multitude thronging thee, and sayest thou, Who touched me?

32   And he looked round about to see her that had done this thing.

33   But the woman fearing and trembling, knowing what was done in her, came and fell down before him, and told him all the truth.

34   And he said unto her, Daughter, thy faith hath made thee whole; go in peace, and be whole of thy plague.

Mark 5:21-34

Occasionally, we make the sad mistake of coming to church and sitting or standing beside the **wrong** person. This tragic mistake can mess up the flow of the Holy Spirit on the entire row. These folks make it difficult for you to press through. They make you work a little harder to receive what God has designed for you. However, there is a way to fix it. There is a way to send a message to every demonic spirit and every negative force that from this point forward, there is absolutely nothing that can be done to distract you or throw you off your pre-determined course. There is nothing anyone or anything can do to keep you from receiving what God has predestined for you. So look at your neighbor, left or right, and repeat my subject after me. Say, "Neighbor, God is going to give me a *Touch to Live.*" If you believe God is going to touch you, you don't have to understand how, when, or where. Just open your mouth and say, "Touch me Lord!"

The narrative of Mark's gospel is a little different from the gospels of Matthew, Luke, and John. For this sermon, I examined Mark's gospel differently than I have before. This time when I studied Mark, I dealt with him as a scholar, not as the theologian or the gospel writer. I wondered what really sets Mark's gospel apart from the other gospel writers of his time. A few things came to mind. One is in the form of a question.

If you were commissioned by God to send a letter of hope to Christians who were inevitably facing certain death, what would you write? Think about that for a minute. What would you write to encourage them? What would you write to give them some sense of hope? Indeed, that is what Mark had to do. He had to write a gospel letter to people who were surely facing death. He had to find a way to communicate hope to people who were in dire need. He chose not to deal with an elaborate introduction of ancestry as Matthew did, and he chose not to entwine himself with the teachings and deeds of Jesus as Luke did. He opted not to get buried deep as John did by conveying Jesus as the very visible form of the invisible God. Mark, rather simply, determined to answer the question by setting up a few other questions.

In his writings, Mark did not bother with the question of whether the reader believed that God and Jesus were one and the same. Instead, Mark begins his letter by suggesting in Chapter 1 that Jesus is God's Son. Whether the reader believed it or not did not affect Mark's writing because he cut straight to the chase giving people who were facing certain death a hope for living. Mark found a way to encourage people who were facing persecution and death because of their faith. Mark accomplishes this feat by concluding that Jesus is the Son of God, and then Mark uses his personal experience with Jesus to describe himself—the writer.

So who is Mark? Who is this person who has the audacity to give us hope when we are feeling the pressures of life? Mark writes his letter out of his own struggles. Personally, it is difficult for me to receive from people who have never struggled through anything. I don't really like folks praying for me who have not been through some experiences of their own. You can suit yourself, but I'd rather know that the person who is laying hands on me is at least sensitive to my struggle. We have all met insensitive Christians. They believe their experiences are the same as everybody else's experiences. They do not realize that though we may share some similarities, we don't come out of the same mold. Just because it was easy for you to give something up is no indication that it is going to be easy for me. I have problems with people who are insensitive or unsympathetic. Please be a little cordial with me as I struggle to live right. Some people assume because you love the Lord and you sing and shout, that you don't have struggles. Let me assure you. Everybody has his or her area of struggle. don't care what kind of title is before your name or after your name! I don't even care how long you have been a Christian. Everybody has struggles.

Mark identifies with people who are tempted to give up under pressure. You may not have seen this fact in your reading of Mark's gospel, but it is there. You have to understand that everybody can't handle pressure. I repeat . . . everybody can't handle pressure. Some of us are a little better at it than others, but pressure is pressure. I don't care how long you've been saved, or how long you've been praying and fasting, or how anointed you think you are, pressure will come your way. At some time in your life, your struggles are going to bring pressure and pressure breeds sleepless nights and insomnia. You may not want to admit it and that's okay, but worry, frustration, aggravation, and anxiety build up from pressure. Mark had to find a way to encourage people who were experiencing pressure.

Mark was familiar with pressure. He was no novice when it came to pressure. During the first missionary journey of Paul and Barnabas, Mark, a young disciple at the time, joined them. The three apostles mapped out a strategic journey. They would leave Jerusalem and pass through Phillister, Lystra and Iconium in order to do God's work in a strange territory. Problems arose at the end of their journey. Paul wanted to go a little further. Barnabas was in agreement, but John Mark said, "Let's go back home. After all, we have finished what we had determined to do. Let's not go any further."

Now, anybody who knows anything about Paul knows that Paul is not one to back up. Paul said, "I'm going on." Barnabas said, "Well, maybe we need to consider what young Mark has said." Paul replies, "I'm not considering anything that Mark has stated. I'm going on." Barnabas then says, "Let's examine." Paul replies, "I'm not considering anything Mark has stated. I'm going on." Barnabas repeats himself, "Let's examine." Then Paul says, "I tell you what, you take Mark and get out. Take Mark and leave." Mark had to deal with the pressure of starting a little confusion between Paul and Barnabas. Adding insult to injury, Barnabas left and took Mark. So you can see that Mark does not write as a novice, or one who had no experience with pressure. He had experienced the pangs of pressure when he was too timid to go on a little further.

I hear the Holy Ghost talking to me right now saying there are some folk sitting here today who are a little timid because you don't know what the next day, moment, hour or week will bring. You are not sure how 1998 will end, but I'm telling you it is better to take a risk. I would rather be known as someone who failed after trying, than someone who didn't try and failed any way. Help me Jesus! Help me in here somebody! I said, I would rather be known as somebody who took a risk and tried and failed, than as somebody who never tried at all.

Mark's story is based on his experience. Let's examine his life quickly. His mother was one of the first converts. She was a Jewish Christian woman who was wealthy and very affluent. She used her home as a base for the Christians to congregate after the Pentecost. At that time, there were no established churches, and Mark's house became a house of prayer. You know those little prayer meetings? Well, Mark's momma opened up one of the first house prayer meetings. The saints would gather there. It was in Mark's house where the saints gathered to pray for Peter after Peter was locked in stocks in the Book of Acts. What Peter writes about in the Book of Acts actually takes place during Mark's time. It was in Mark's momma's house where folks gathered to pray for the Apostle Peter's release. Recall the story where the damsel answered the door and it was Peter knocking on the door. She got so excited that she forgot to open the door. Instead, she ran back inside and said to the others, "Everyone, get up, Peter is at the door." They replied, "Nah, Peter is in the jail." She said, "No, Peter is at the door." She ran back and opened the door and in walks Peter. All of that scripture happened in Mark's momma's house.

Let me digress here for a moment. It is difficult for me to understand how a person can say he or she loves God, and yet, they have no relationship with God. Somewhere in your knowing God, you have to experience Him. Too many folks don't personally know God. Maybe that is the reason we have so much trouble with some people. Maybe, we have unintentionally denied folks the leeway to learn God for themselves. Maybe folks have been propped up and pacified for so long that they find it difficult to stand on their own two feet. Maybe we need to just back up and let you do your own praying. Maybe we should let you do your own fasting and struggling because if you struggle with it long and hard enough, you won't need as much help to get you out of your mess. Maybe you have not struggled through because we made it too easy for you not to struggle. Maybe we have had too many prayer services and laid our hands on you too many times. Maybe we need to back up and let you look at yourself in the mirror and lay your hands on your own self. Maybe we should just back up and let you pray for yourself. Maybe you are banking too much on what I know about God. Maybe it is about time you develop and learn through your own experiences with God.

Let us return to Mark. Mark was no novice about the things of God. He wrote about what he had heard. He wrote about what he had seen. He wrote from his own personal experiences. In fact, Mark wrote under the pressures of that time, demonstrating that no matter what difficulties we face in life, we have a Savior we can touch. No matter how rough or tough it might get, we have a Savior we can touch. That is what Mark says. Not only do we have a Savior we can touch, we have a Savior who is moved by our touch. We have a Savior who understands when we try to touch Him and He is moved by our trying. Lastly, we have a Savior who can touch us back.

There is a dialogue in Mark which clearly demonstrates just how sensitive Jesus is toward His people. Mark reveals how sensitive the Lord is to someone who is trying to touch Him. Therein lays the background for our text. The scene from our text begins with a father named Jairus asking Jesus to heal his sick daughter. Let me set the scene for you. Jesus has traveled over the sea of Gasaria and has returned to His own town. He gets off the boat with the disciples following Him, and there is a ruler of the synagogue by the name of Jairus who runs out to meet Him. Jairus falls down at Jesus' feet. He begins to lament. He says, "Jesus, my daughter is sick. She is sick unto death."

I can only imagine this father's dilemma over a daughter who he loves . . . a daughter who is dying. I can compare it to the relationship between my husband, Bishop, and my daughter, Kristel. I have watched my husband with my daughter. I have seen the gleam in Kristel's eye when her father walks into the room. I have watched as she and I leave the house and she hollers, "Front seat!" just so she can sit close to her daddy. I can only imagine the pain that would grip Bishop's heart if Kristel were lying on a bed sick and there was absolutely nothing he could do to ease her pain or to stop her illness. I can only imagine the heartbreak that would fill his heart to watch his baby girl, the one he loves, wrapped up in a blanket of pain. I have seen him hold her and pray for her. I can only imagine how his heart would break watching Kristel's fever rise night and day and be helpless to help her. I can only imagine the pain that would fill his mind knowing that there is no doctor in town or no medicine he could buy to stop her illness.

So can you imagine how Jairus must have felt when he saw Jesus? He must have been thinking, "Here is someone who can help me." No wonder he ran and fell down at Jesus' feet. My God from Zion! It didn't matter that he was dressed up. It didn't matter that he was a ruler. For once in his life, there was hope coming across the sea. He had heard about this man called Jesus. He had heard the songs which were sung about this man. He had heard all of the testimonies concerning Jesus. Jairus did not hesitate to fall down at the feet of Jesus.

Let's examine the text. Not only did Jairus fall down at Jesus' feet and petition Him to heal his daughter, but the Bible says Jairus begs Him. It is in the book. Read it. He begs. Let me paraphrase the ruler's comments. He says, "I do not care how busy you are. I do not know why you came here. I do not understand what you have to do, but I have a girl who is sick unto death. My hands are tied and there is nothing I can buy or no potion I can give her to make her well. I need you please! I know you do not know her. I know you do not have to do what I ask, but she is my daughter. I love her. Please!" "Help me," he begs. "Jesus, please do not send an apostle. Do not speak the word. She is too precious to me. I cannot put her in anybody's hands, but yours. You are my last hope. If you cannot make her well, I will prepare for her burial, but I am begging you to do it for me." Can you imagine the scene? Can you see Jairus? Can you see the frustration and the tears? Can you understand his agony? He had never met Jesus. Jesus could have turned him down. He had no indication whether Jesus was going to come with him, but he kept on crying, "Please, you can do it if you want to. I am begging you. Touch her."

This narrative leads me to my first point which is Jesus can be touched. No matter what you are dealing with or who has set himself or herself against you, Jesus can be touched. I know He can because in the next verse Jesus says to Jairus, "Where do you live? Take me to your house." Can you see Jairus wiping his tears, jumping up from the ground, and grabbing Jesus by the hand saying, "Please sir? I'll take you to my house." What did Jairus do? Jairus made a point of contact with Jesus. Some of you before you leave here today are going to get an opportunity to touch Jesus. It does not matter who is sitting next to you. It does not matter who invited you to Calvary. You may be visiting this morning or you may be a member of this church and decided to come out of duty, but whatever the reason, you are here. There is a point of contact where you can actually touch Jesus. You can touch Him by crying. You can touch Him by praying. You can touch Him through singing. You can touch Him through praise, and God knows you can touch Him through worship. But you can touch Him. Look at your neighbor and say, "Neighbor, I'm going to touch Him before I leave today. I'm going to reach beyond my problem and the pressure I'm dealing with and find a way to touch Jesus."

Jesus asks Jairus, "Where do you live? Where is your house?" Can you see Jairus with a spring in his step? He understands that his daughter is sick, but Jesus is on the way. Can you imagine the pitter-patter in his heart and the joy that filled his mind? "My God! Jesus said He is going to come. Jesus is coming to my house." Can you imagine how he felt? For the first time in months, he has a ray of hope for his daughter. She can get well. Can you see him as he's marching? He has Jesus by the hand. The Bible says a crowd had gathered because Jesus was in town. Wherever Jesus went, people came from everywhere to see

10

Him. However, Jairus is not focused on the crowd; he is steadily moving towards his house. "If I can just get Jesus to my house . . ." Can you see Jairus holding onto Jesus' hand? He maneuvers his way through and around the crowd and the crowd is following Jesus and Jairus. Jairus did not lose his focus and he was not distracted. There were people all around him, but for the first time in many days, he had hope of healing for his little girl. She was just twelve years old. She was too young to die now. As the crowd continues to grow, Jairus has Jesus by the hand. Eventually, the multitude surrounds Jairus, but he is still holding on to Jesus.

Let me tell you something. Jesus will never touch some of you because you give up too quickly. You let go too soon. You get too distracted by the folk around you. But what you <u>need</u> to do is forget about who is on your left and right and reach out and touch Jesus.

Imagine how quickly Jairus tried to move Jesus. "Come on Jesus. We have to hurry up." While they maneuvered through the crowd, something happens which distracts Jesus. There is a little lady in the crowd who had suffered with a blood disease for twelve years. She has exhausted all her money and no doctor in or out of town could cure the infection. She is in the crowd and it is her last chance. If she does not get to Jesus now, chances are she will die soon. She makes up her mind that one way or another; she was going to get to Jesus. She realizes the crowd is growing, but she is determined to reach Jesus. She is weak and weary. She is filthy and stinking, but she believes this chance is her last. But how? Jairus won't let go of Jesus! She says to herself, "If Jairus would just loose

Jesus' hand, maybe I can get to Him." If he would just let go of Jesus, but Jairus does not let Jesus go. The lady decides, "If I can just touch His hand or grab hold of His clothes." So the lady prostrates herself on the ground in the middle of the crowd.

It makes a difference when you lay yourself down. Some of you stand up too much. You need to learn how to throw yourself on the floor and stay there! You need to learn how to get down on the floor and let your children see you on the floor. Go ahead, waddle and roll, but stay there.

So this woman gets down on the ground and she starts crawling. She did not say anything to anybody. She came close enough to grab Jesus' skirt. She grabbed the robe and she held onto it. She did just what Jairus had done. She held that coat and did not open her mouth. Jairus cried, but she held on. Do I have some folk in here who are tired of crying, but you're still holding on? In His name, I'm holding on. I'm on my last leg, but I'm holding on. The lady grabbed Jesus' robe, but Jairus would not let go. Jesus turned around and said to the disciples, "Who touched me?" Can you imagine Jairus thinking, "Come on, Jesus. Don't worry about it. It's all right. There are a whole lot of folk here." Then the disciples said out loud what Jairus had been thinking. They said, "Lord, we know you are not asking us, in the midst of these thousands of people, who touched you? Forget about it and keep moving on." Jairus said, "Yea, let's forget about it and let's keep on moving." Jesus stopped dead center and said, "No. This was not an ordinary touch. It was not a 'Hi' or 'How do you do touch?' It was not an admiring touch, but somebody touched me out of a need." Do I have some folk in here who don't know why you came out today, but you are going to get a touch for your own need? Do I have some folk saying, "I know she doesn't know my business, but I have a need. I don't know why I'm here, but thank God, God is going to touch me. God is going to deliver me!"

Jesus said it was a touch that required virtue and He knew every time virtue left His body. Can you imagine Jairus trying to move Jesus onward? But Jesus wouldn't move. The woman, fearing and trembling, stood up and said, "Sir, it was I." Let me tell you what caught my eye about her statement. She did not move out of eye contact with Jesus. Some of you have moved too far away from Jesus. You need to get back into eye contact with Jesus. I repeat . . . some of you have moved too far away from Jesus. You need to get into eye contact with Jesus. You need to see where Jesus wants you to go.

Jairus is standing there. The woman has given Jesus her testimony. By the time she gets through talking, someone from Jairus' house tells him he might as well forget it now. It is too late. Your daughter has just died. Your girl is gone. Go on home and try to console your wife. Your house is in a frenzy. Can you imagine Jairus standing there beside Jesus and receiving the news that it was too late? All of your efforts now mean nothing. You might as well give it up. You might as well let it go. You might as well go back where you came from because there is no help for your little girl. She is already dead. Can you imagine what gripped him? In his mind he was probably thinking, "I tried so hard. Why did she die? Why couldn't you come? Why did you stop to talk to that woman? I told you my girl was sick." But Jesus whispers in Jairus' ear, "Be not afraid, just believe." My God from Zion! Don't be afraid just keep on believing. Keep on believing. This time, Jesus takes Jairus' hand and says, "Now, show me where you live." Until then, Jairus had held on to Jesus' hand, but this time, Jesus grabs Jairus' hand and says, "Come on, show me—just show me—just show me where you live!" Bless the name of God! Jesus says to the crowd, "Don't go any further." He says to Peter, James, and John, "You come with me."

Look at your neighbor and say, "I need someone with me who doesn't mind being touched." If you are too tired, or too full, sit down. I need somebody around me who is not afraid to be touched. I need someone around me who can believe all things are possible if I believe it. I need two or three folk surrounding me who believe "greater is He who is in me." I need folk who believe that no weapon formed against me shall prosper, who believe that all things are working together for my good, and who believe I am more than a conquer. Say yes! Say yes! Bless His name.

Jesus arrives at the house and says to Jairus, "Come with me." They enter in the room. Can you see the scene? Jairus' wife is on the bedside saying "What took you so long? They told me you had Jesus and that you were coming. There is nothing we can do. She is already dead. We might as well wrap her up and give her to the mortician." Jairus is just standing there, not knowing what to say. All he knows is what Jesus just told him. But he is looking at a dead girl with no life in her body.

That is my last point. Some of you need to be touched at the dead place. You need to be touched at the place where there is no life. You need to be touched at the place where you stopped shouting. You need to be touched at the place where you stopped praying. You need to be touched at the place where you stopped believing. You need to be touched at the place where you stopped worshipping. You need to be touched in the dead place. I know you don't want to admit it, but you are here today with a dead place. You're at the place where the doctor gave up on you. You're at the place where your momma gave up on you. You're at a dead place. Lean on somebody and tell them, "I'm going to praise Him at a dead place." I am going to give Him glory at the dead place. I am going to shout it out at the dead place. Bless the name of God.

The Bible says that Jesus looked at Jairus. Jairus said, "I believe." Then the Bible says that Jesus stepped back and called the girl by her name. When she arose He said, "Feed her." Any time you've been dead, the next thing you need to do is get something to eat. Some of you have been dead so long; you don't know what a good meal taste like! I'm going to give you a moment to clap your hands and to stomp your feet and let you feel what the joy of the Lord will do. I'm going to give you a minute to touch Jesus, so that Jesus can touch you back. I'm glad we have a High Priest who can be touched with our infirmities. I'm glad I have a God who knows how I feel. He knows what I am going through. The Bible says that Jairus took the girl up and they fed her. Jesus left, and He told them not to tell anybody because His time was not yet. But when Jesus touches you, you don't have to tell it.

Your hands look new. Your feet look new. Something seeps into your heart and causes your body to feel new.

Is there anybody in here who needs to be touched? Do I have anybody in here that needs a touch of life? I am not talking about a feel good touch. I'm talking about a touch that will give you life. I'm talking about a touch that will make you get up, look the devil in the face, and say, "You meant it for evil. You tried to kill me with it. You tried to destroy me. You meant it for evil, but I am going to show you. You messed with my children, you messed with my money, and you tried to mess with me. I am going to show you that what you meant for evil, I'm going to take it and praise Jesus in the middle of it." You can bless Jesus before He touches you. You can give Him the glory even before He fixes the mess. You can shout while you are still hurting. You can praise Him while you're still broken. You can say "yes" to His word. Say yes!

I need about a hundred folks who do not care what is going on in their lives to praise Him right now. I may not have any money. I don't care if it is almost Christmas and I don't have any charge cards I can use. I will not get depressed and I will not get upset. I will show the devil that whatever I need, Jesus has it. He has everything I need. I am going to stretch myself out and lay down in front of Jesus. I'm going to ask Him to touch me one more time. I am going to ask Him to touch me at my dead place and to touch me at the place where I am hurting. He can touch me where my heart is broken. He can touch me where my mind is messed up. He can bring me peace. I may have to step out from this row. I may have to turn around in the middle of the floor and do the Boogaloo, but I'm going to do what I need to do because

I need a touch of life. I may have to run up and down the aisles of the church. I may have to skip across the pulpit, but I will do whatever is necessary because I need a touch of life. I need a touch so I can live, so I will live and not die. I must live. I have come too far. I have given up too much. I must live. I'm going to dance so I can live. Some of you may clap, some of you may holler, others may scream and some of you may run, but do whatever you have to do because this praise is going to bring a touch from God. This praise is like the woman with the issue of blood. This praise is like Jairus' praise.

At one point, I thought I was going to kill myself. I felt like taking my own life, but I felt God. He touched me. He made it better. I must live. I've <u>got</u> to live. Do what you have to do, but live! The devil wanted me to die. The devil -- he is a liar! He tried to distract me and get me off focus all during the week. On Thanksgiving Day I felt so low, I didn't want to see. I didn't want to be. But I felt God working on me. I must live. I hear the Holy Ghost saying, this time touch three people, look them dead center in the face and tell them, "God said you will live." You are coming through. She's getting up. You're getting out. Trust me, what you're going through is not going to kill you. It will not destroy you. I know it may be broke, but you will live. I know the situation is all messed up, but you will live. I know things may be falling down around you, but you will live. I know you are hurting, but you will live. I know you are crying, but you will live. I know you're messed up, but you will live. Say LIVE!

The Bible does not mention the ensuing reaction, but can you imagine the scene when news of the daughter's miraculous recovery from death got out? Momma told grandma. Grandma told grandpa. Grandpa told the aunt. The aunt told the uncle, the cousins, and the nieces. Can you imagine the excitement that filled their hearts? This girl was not dead because Jesus raised her up. Can you imagine how happy they were every time they passed the bed in which she had died?

The moral of this story is this: Just because Jesus is detained, doesn't mean He is not coming. Sometimes you must provoke a blessing. So until He gets here, I will celebrate right where I am. I will celebrate until He gets here. Because when He gets here, everything will be all right. I have a touch on the way. I have life on the way. I am getting ready to make every devil in hell jump back. I am getting ready to make every demonic spirit flee from me. I am getting ready to put the devil under my foot through living and praising Jesus. I will celebrate what Jesus is **going** to do. He may have been detained, but I am not denied. I must celebrate Him. You must celebrate Him. Celebrate by yourself if you have to. You don't need anybody to help you celebrate Him. Once you realize Jesus is almost at your house and once you sense His presence is coming near, you don't need anybody to help you celebrate Him. I do not need you to open your mouth. I can dance by myself. I can jump by myself. I can praise Him all by myself.

The girl died while everyone was waiting for Jesus. Jesus tried to get to her. What Jairus did not understand at the time is that the one he was holding on to – Jesus – was life itself. What you need to understand is that the one who is holding on to you is life Himself. There is no way you can die when the Master has your hand. Sometimes

He takes care of somebody else while He is holding on to you. Jesus is big enough to take care of you and still hold on to me. Thank you, Jesus! He is strong enough to see about you and still hold on to me.

Bow your head and close your eyes. Slip your hand in someone else's hand. Thank you, Jesus. God, I know there are brothers and sisters all over this room who think they have no reason to go on. They feel life pulling at them with so much pressure that they don't know which way to go. They feel like Jairus. They don't realize that if You said You were coming it doesn't matter when You get there. You can take care of everything once You are there. I ask you, Father, to shower down a touch of life. Touch our minds. Touch our hearts and our spirits. Touch our bodies and our emotions. Touch situations and circumstances. We are provoking a blessing. Lord, be touched by what we say. Be touched by our tears, Lord. Be touched by our praise. At our dead places, touch us. Where we lie dying, touch us. Now lift up your heads and lift up your hearts and feel His presence.

We are holding onto a hand and we don't know what they need Lord, but we know You have the power to touch. Fill their hearts with joy. Let my hand be the hand of Jesus. Let my grip be the grip of the hand of God. Just like you grabbed Jairus, grab my sister. Touch my brother. You said if two or three of us would touch and agree, you would be in the midst. Do it even now, dear Father. Help us feel better about ourselves. Help us feel better about what we are dealing with and going through. Help us to understand that if we lean not on our own understanding, You will work things out right on schedule. Help us to understand everything will be all right. We thank You. We praise You. Keep those eyes closed. Lift up your hands and worship the Lord.

I'm Going Further Than This

7   And the LORD said unto Joshua, This day will I begin to magnify thee in the sight of all Israel, that they may know that, as I was with Moses, so I will be with thee.

8   And thou shalt command the priests that bear the ark of the covenant, saying, When ye are come to the brink of the water of Jordan, ye shall stand still in Jordan.

9   And Joshua said unto the children of Israel, Come hither, and hear the words of the LORD your God.

Joshua 3:7-9

Let's go to Joshua 3 and look at verses 7, 8, and 9. Look at your neighbor, eyeball to eyeball, and repeat my subject after me. Say, "Neighbor, today Co-Pastor is going to talk about going further than this." Look at the neighbor on the other side, and say it just like me, say "Neighbor, oh neighbor, *I'm Going Further Than This.*" Throw your hands up so the enemy will know that no matter what position or situation you're in right now, you're getting ready to go further. Say "Devil, I want you to know, *I'm going further than this.*"

We will begin today's discussion by setting up the textual structure of the story. I do not have time to go into all of the dynamics which allowed Joshua to assume the leadership of the children or the tribes of Israel. I'm not going to spend a lot of time developing the backdrop of the text. However, I will tell you that some consecrated activity lead to Joshua taking over the headship of the nation of Israel, and it's necessary to dialogue just a bit in order to understand what propelled Joshua into the position he is in at the time of the text.

First of all, Moses is dead at the timing of our text. You all know Moses from Sunday School 101. He was the great deliverer God used to get the Jewish people out of Egyptian bondage. The fact that Moses was dead is important. Moses' life and leadership were exemplary, but at the time of our text, he was dead. The great deliverer was no longer. The great deliverer, who had such a good relationship and fellowship with God, was gone. Moses was not there. So you must understand that sometimes, when you begin walking into your purpose and into your destiny, you must find the strength to go on despite the fact that what you counted on for strength before is no longer there.

Let's just park there a moment. If you're going to progress with God, you must learn this lesson and learn it well. If it's dead, no matter how good it was, it's over. See, some folk think they only need to let bad things be buried, but sometimes even good things must be buried. Lord, have mercy! What was good for you today or yesterday may not be in your best interest tomorrow or the next day. Where my folk at . . . where my folk? I said it may not be in your best interest on tomorrow. So no matter how good Moses was in leading the Jews out of bondage and to the place where they are at the time of our text, that time was over. Moses is dead. Look at somebody and tell them, "It's over!" No matter what you went through, how you got through, why you got through, or who got you through, it is over. You have to let it go.

I came to help a few folk today in the Nation of Calvary. Some of you sisters and brothers have been nursing some dead situations. We have people who nurse dead promises. We have folk who sit in the church and hold grudges because the person on the left side of the church borrowed $500 from them and it has been three years and they have not paid you back. Well, if they have not paid you back by now, get over it, honey! You have lived. You are living. You are still making it. You are not broke. Get over it and let it go! Slap somebody a five and say, "Let it go – let it go!" It's dead, dead, dead! Yet you're still holding on to it. Just nursing that hurt. The thing is dead. Let it go! If you don't like me, you just don't like me. I'm going to park my little tail right next to yours, sit on that row, and have a good time while you're going through. I'm not going to let you kill me! Honey, I will take a handkerchief and the Bible and dance right on your little dead self. I will dance right over you while you sit there trying to figure out why I'm dancing.

I know scientists are trying to freeze folk free. They are trying to freeze people! I say if you're dead, let's call it through. Who knows what you will look like when they unfreeze you? I don't know what your eyes will look like. I don't know what your toenails will look like. So I say if you are dead, let's chalk it up. Dead things eventually start stinking. Oh, you don't want to hear any preaching. I said dead stuff will start to stink! Why would you want to hold on to something that will eventually mess you up? If it doesn't mess you up, it will cause you to smell like you are messed up. Why would you hang around with folk that are in and out of the church and can't get themselves straight with God? After a while, you will start to look and smell funny too. Where are my folk? Where my folk at?

You must make up your mind, "I'm going to the next level and I am not taking anything or anybody with me who don't want to go!" Just leave me alone and get out of my world!

So no matter how good Moses' leadership was, he was dead at the time of our text. Israel had to stop focusing on Moses and they had to start paying attention to Joshua. I had to bring this point to your understanding. Sometimes, God will allow something to die in order to bring you to a turning point. Some of you will never move to the next level because you're trying to hold on to something that God only meant to be temporary. Who am I talking to in here? God didn't mean for that job to be permanent, but you wouldn't look for another one, so He let the boss fire your butt because He had to bring you to a turning point! Some of you will never look for the next level God has ordained for your life because you're too busy being comfortable in the position that you are in now. Slap your neighbor a five and say, "Move on. Move on. Move on!" God had to let Moses die. I'm going to move on after this point. Moses was too old. He did not have the strength nor the know how to fight in Canaan. Now, I did not say that Moses wasn't good. Moses was good. Moses was real good. He was the deliverer. His momma hid him in the water and everything. He was good! However, it was not his assignment to go into Canaan and fight and conquer the land.

I came for somebody in here today. God knows I came to coach you into your next move with God. I came to push you and to tell you, you can do it. You can make it. Forget about Moses and look to the future. God will use you to get you where He wants you to be. It is now

Joshua's time. I'm talking to somebody. You have to tell yourself, "This is my time." If you have to get in front of the mirror and say it from now 'til December 31, just repeat it over and over, "It's my time." If you don't say it, you won't have it. You must tell yourself, "It is my time. I've been prepared for this time. I'm positioned for this time." Slap three people a five and say, "My time!" I'll walk all over you. It's my time! I believe it's my time! You don't have to believe it's my time. I did not ask you to believe it's my time. You don't have to send me a card, give me a telegram, or e-mail me. I said, it's MY TIME . . . where my folk at? I may not have a dime in the bank right now, but it is my time. Say yes! Say yes! Say yes!

God has already set things up for you, but He is waiting for you to say something. He will not release it until you say it. The scripture says what a man thinks in his heart, so is he. Lord, have mercy. If you don't think you will ever live in a five bedroom house with a bathroom in every bedroom, then you won't live in one. If you are satisfied driving that "Hoopty," then that is what you are going to drive. But I dare you to get up in the morning and say "Mercedes --black or silver -- the car is mine." Dance because it is yours. Slap that neighbor on the shoulder and tell them "It's a matter of time, but it is mine." Lord, I may not be driving it right now, but it's a matter of time. Honey, that car is mine. Make a declaration that today is the day. Stop wishful thinking and make some things happen. Who am I talking to? Faith without works is dead. Get up and <u>do</u> something.

You have been sitting on that row, service after service, affirming everybody else. "Girl, I'm so glad the

Lord blessed you." No! I'm tired of Him blessing you. I'm getting ready to turn this place out if I don't get a blessing up in here. I said I'm going to turn this place inside out! I'm going to run up and down these aisles. I'm going to prostrate myself on the floor. I may be in here all night by myself, but I'm going to get something. I'm not waiting until I get to heaven to get everything God has for me. The devil is a big lie. He's a big lie. I won't need a car in heaven – I'll have wings!

Don't tell me anything about "wishful thinking" because I am not wishful thinking. The wealth of the wicked is already laid up for me. I just got to tap into it. So do you. Some of you will not get anything because you do not prophesy to yourself. You are waiting for somebody to come in here and prophesy to you. You better learn how to prophesy to your own self. Where my folk at, where are my folk? It's not a matter of whether we deserve it or not. We don't deserve anything. You don't deserve anything. I don't deserve anything. God just gives it to us anyway.

Some of you ministers here today don't say anything about what God is doing for you. That's why nobody believes in you, because you don't say anything. You are too busy talking about Daniel in the lion's den, the Hebrew boys in the fiery furnace, and all that stuff. Folks need to know what God is doing for you! So if I drive a Cadillac truck and Bishop drives a Mercedes and Mooky drives a truck and Crystal drives a Mercedes, don't say anything to me. Don't say anything to me because I will tell you that we are driving those cars because the Lord has blessed us. God has an ego and anytime you start talking about how good God is to you, God will do what He says. That's why you don't have anything because you

26

are not saying anything. Lord, have mercy! You are too busy apologizing. If you were blessed with a new house, put it on the video! "On July the 9th, the wife and I signed our mortgage. We signed it. My wife and I, the kids, and the dog… all of us are in the new house."

God wants you to make mention of what He is doing for you and He is not going to do any more for you until you start talking about what He has already done. It only becomes arrogant and boastful when you don't give God the credit. But if I stand up here and say we are blessed because God has blessed us and we're living well because God has blessed us, and I give God all the glory. God will show up and show out! So I give Him all the praise. I give Him all the thanks because if it had not been for Him, I would have nothing. But since He decided to bless me . . . Lord, have mercy! I need somebody to praise Him for what you already have. Slap that neighbor a five and say, "I'm going further than this!" Just think of me as your coach. I'm your coach. I'm going to push somebody into a brand new day.

Now, let's go back to the text. If Joshua is going to lead Israel from one side of the Jordan, through the Jordan, and to what God had promised, he will need two things. He needs to be strong and he needs to be courageous. This last move of God is not for weak people. If you are worried about what people will think and if you are worried about what people will say, then you might as well sit down. Because as sure as He starts blessing you, somebody is going to have something to say. You must know that everybody will not be happy for you. They will not be happy for you because they really want your blessing. That little jealous spirit that is inside of them will take over and they will wonder how you got what you have. So you must be strong. You will have to set your faith like flint, and you will need to remove anybody from your world who is not for you. So some of you will have to cut some ties when you leave here today. Anybody who is dragging you down and does not want you to get your blessing, please get rid of them.

You cannot be weak and handle the blessings of the Lord. Lord, help me. I said, you cannot be a weak person and handle the abundance of God! You have to be strong and Joshua became real strong. He said, "As for me and my house, we will serve the Lord." I don't know about the rest of you. I don't care about the rest of you. But as for me and my house, we will serve the Lord. Whatever God has lined up for me, I'm going to get. You must be strong and you have to be courageous. You've got to be willing to take some kind of risk. You've got to be courageous. You cannot be scared.

You cannot walk to the next level God is taking this church if you are scared. Folks are going to talk about us. "Who do they think they are over there -- in -- in the Ghetto? Who do they think they are -- buying up all that property? Who do they think they are?" They will wonder, "Where they getting the money from?" We are not doing anything but praising God and calling those things that are not as though they were. We are over here saying, "God, whenever you get ready to pour it out, here we are." You've got to be courageous. You've got to have courage to believe in yourself, to stay strong, and to walk with God, so when the promises of God are released, you are right in line. I don't want God to start releasing the promises and I'm in the back of the line! Not the back of the line! I want to be somewhere in the middle or towards the front. Not the back! Do you know how long it takes people at the back of the line to get to the front? Honey, get yourself situated and stationed so that when God opens up the windows of heaven and starts pouring out the blessings, you are right there up front.

Joshua could not afford to be scared. He had to be courageous. If the promise of God is over there, then you've got to get over there. If you have to skip over somebody, jump past somebody, or walk over somebody, if you see the promise, get over there! Tell your neighbor, "Get over there!" If you don't hurry up and get there, I'm going to get yours and mine too.

Do you know that some people start apologizing when God starts blessing them? That is an insult to God. If God opens up a door and makes a way for you and you start apologizing, you're insulting God. Don't you know it's not about you? It's never about you. It's about God! You've got to be careful so that when life begins turning around for you, you don't let people put you in a predicament. Folks will put you in a predicament and mess up your promise. You cannot make good decisions when you are in a predicament. Joshua got strong and Joshua got courageous while he was looking at the Jordan. He didn't wait until he got in the middle of the Jordan; he became strong and courageous while he was looking at the water. Tell your neighbor, "While you are looking for the blessing, give God the glory for the blessing." Let's say it another way. Grab your neighbor by the hand and shake it a little bit and say, "Neighbor, I will get there because I'm

29

going further." Clap your hands and let me hear you praise Him. I'll get there, honey. I will get there. It may take me the next four months, but I will get there. I may be ten years skipping around it, but I will get there!

Joshua decides that he will cross the Jordan. Now he has one or two choices. He could either settle for what God has already done or use faith and move where he thinks God will do something else. Let me prove it. Israel was in a good place. God had fed them, water came out of the rock, quails flew over, and they had meat. Wafers and bread came out of the earth. It was a good place, but it was not their promised possession. I'm coaching somebody. If you're not careful, you will settle at the good place, not realizing that the good place is not your promised possession. Who am I talking to in here today? Lord, help me preach. You must keep your eyes, focus, and vision on <u>all</u> of the promise. Say, "ALL of the promise." You may be living good right now, driving good right now, eating good right now, and wearing good right now, but that is not all that God promised. You've got to go further than this. I am going to push you to your new place, but as I push you to the new place, you will have to activate your faith to get there. I can push you, but I can't make you receive it. You can have all the faith that you want, but faith without works is dead. Who am I talking to up in here today?

Joshua's dilemma is that his assignment is not only to get himself across the Jordan, but he has two million folk to get across, too. I'm trying to set this up for you. If you're going to go to the next level, you may have to pull somebody with you. Here is the clincher: when he looked at the Jordan, the water, according to the text, was overflowing its banks. He has to get himself and two million folk across a river that is out of control. I don't know who I came for today, but I came to coach you. Sometimes when you make up your mind that you are going to move to the next level, everything and everybody in your life gets out of control. Who am I preaching to in here today? Lord, have mercy! Everything gets out of control. No money. Loans are not coming through. Don't know which way to turn. Don't know whom to ask. Everything is out of control. You have to make up your mind while the wind is blowing, while the waves are crashing, and while the storm is raging, that where I am today is not the end of my story. Grab your neighbor by the hand and shake it a little bit. Say, "Neighbor, I got a situation, everything is out of control, but I'm making a declaration today that I'm going further and this is not the end of my story." I need somebody to praise Him right here. I said I need to hear something in here! I need to hear you buck against the gates of hell. I need to hear you bring down the perimeters of poverty. I need to hear you shout "It's not the end of my story!"

Joshua looks at the Jordan. It is in the text. The river banks were overflowing. He has got to come up with a way to get across. Let's examine verses 5 through 10. You must know that none of this message is going to work for you, if you are not clean. There is no sense in you making a declaration to anything or anybody if you are sinning. I don't care what kind of sin you are doing. Before Joshua did anything, he said "sanctify." Sanctification is not a long dress, a hat, and a three-piece suit. Sanctification is how you walk with God on a daily basis. Where my folk? I need my folk for real. If you think God is going to open up the windows of Heaven and give you all this stuff and you are deep in sin, you are crazy! So Joshua said, "Before we move over the Jordan, before we take hold of any possessions, before we receive any promises, we've got to get cleaned up.

That is my first point. You've got to get cleaned up. God has promised to bless us and not curse us. He has promised to make us the first -- the head and not the tail. He has promised we would be the lenders and not the borrowers. He is not going to open up Heaven and release any promise to you while you are living like the devil. If you think the Lord is going to do wonders for you, you better know you are clean. If you're clean before this year is out, God will do some wonders.

My second point is there is some stuff God is going to give to you in plain sight of those folk who said you would not have anything. Where my folk? He will give you stuff in front of those family members at the family reunion who laughed at you and called you a "holy roller." He will do some of this stuff to magnify you in the presence of your enemies. He will magnify you in front of folk. I don't care what the supervisor said. God will rearrange a whole office and completely destroy a whole organization, just to magnify you in front of your enemies! Is there anybody who believes it?

Joshua sanctified himself and gave himself a position, but the position was affirmed right there in the scripture. It says ye shall know that the living God is among you and that He will not fail. You got to know that as you begin to go further, God is going to do everything that He said He was going to do without fail! I know it is a little rough right here, so turn around and tell three people, "Without fail! I will get it." I'm going to have it without fail. Without fail! I'm coming out without fail. It will get better without fail. God will release it without fail. I will cross this river without fail. I'm coming out of this place without fail. I'm going to get over it without fail. I'll break it loose because God said I will do it without fail.

This proclamation changes the point of victory because now Joshua is going to get the people across Jordan without fail. Once he positioned himself and the people began to sanctify themselves, he opened up a way for God to do what God wanted to do without fail. Now, how many of you believe that God has to make good on His word? I'm coaching somebody right here. God has to make good on His word. God has to do it if He spoke it for you. He may have to fool around with you and take you through some things to help you get where He wants you to be. He may have to spank you, turn you around, cut you loose, let somebody lie on you, let you lose it, let you get it, let you lose it, and let you get it. He may have to work with you a little while, but if He said it! I don't care if every loan company you went to said you didn't qualify, if God spoke it, it will happen. You might as well get yourself some coffee and sit yourself down because before they say, "ashes to ashes and dust to dust." Where my folk at? I've got to get it because God said it. I got to have it because God spoke it. It's got to get better because God promised! Joshua positioned himself because God said, "Without fail." I know the river is overflowing. I know that there are enemies in the land, but without fail, you are going to cross this Jordan. Joshua decides not only must

33

he position himself, he must allow God's presence to go first.

Let's examine verses five and six. While they were in the wilderness coming out of Egypt, God's presence was visible. It was a cloud by day and fire by night. So the presence of the Lord was signified in the cloud and in the fire. But at this next level, you must symbolically take the presence. In other words, you have to take Him when you can't see Him. Some of you are used to having God nearby. You can praise Him as long as you can see Him, as long as you can see the way being made, as long as you can see deliverance, or as long as you can sense folk like you. Do I have anybody who wants to go further? In this next level, you have to symbolically take Him. In other words, you have to believe He is with you when He is not working it out. You have to believe you are going to get it when you don't see any way being made to have it. You have to believe you are well when the doctor says you're sick. You have to take Him with you symbolically. In other words, you have to know what you know. Slap your neighbor five and tell them, "I know I'm going further."

Israel took the Arc of the Covenant and the tablets of stone in it and Aaron's rod and gave it to the priest. They gave it to the priest and they said "Go before us." Pass over the Jordan before us. When the Arc was ready to be moved, the priest said "Get you somebody who wants to go with you." Ask your neighbor, "Do you want to go with me today?" If they didn't respond right away, you better turn around and find somebody who is talking like they want to go where you are going. I made up my mind I will not have anybody in my life that doesn't believe what I believe. If you don't believe I'm going to get it, get out of my way. Just get out of my way! Don't bother me, and don't ask me any questions. I don't want to ride in your car. I don't want to eat lunch with you. I don't want to do anything with you if you don't believe what I believe because I believe I'm going to have whatever I desire.

If I say He is a way maker and I have enough courage to believe it, then I'm going to have it! I'm going to do just like those lepers in II Kings 7:4. They said, "We have nothing, why should we sit here?" I don't have anything now, but why should I sit here and condemn myself? If I just get up, maybe it will come while I'm walking. I just need somebody to start walking – start walking – start walking. That is what the priest did. They took the Arc of the Covenant and they started walking. They walked into the water. They walked, they walked, and they kept on walking. The more they walked, the more the water receded. I'm talking about water that was overflowing.

Now you must understand that these folks were not the bunch who saw the Red Sea part. The folks who saw the Red Sea part were the mothers and fathers of the folks crossing the Jordan. So crossing the Jordan was not something they were doing because they had seen it done before. I'm talking to somebody who has never seen it happen before. I mean your momma didn't get blessed, your daddy didn't get blessed, your big momma didn't get blessed, and nobody in your family has been blessed like you think you are going to be blessed. You have never seen it happen! Lord, have mercy! I have never seen anybody get healed from cancer. My momma died of breast cancer. My grand momma died of cancer and now you telling me I have cancer, but I got to walk into healing. I have never seen it happen, but if I just walk in it. If I can just put my foot in the water, maybe the Lord will make a way. Who am I talking to? I dare you to jump up and go to walking. I got to step out. I may fall. I may stumble. Folks may laugh at me but I got to walk it. I got to walk it. Slap your neighbor a five as you take your seat, and say, "Neighbor, I got to walk it. I have nothing to loose. I am going further." Say yes!

These folks are the second generation of Israelites. They don't know anything about water backing up, but when the priest walked, the water began to recede. The text is clear and I looked it up in two or three commentaries and two other translations. It did not say the water disappeared. Go home and read it. When they walked, the water backed up. Which means you must walk in the face of whatever. Lord, have mercy! It's easy to walk when there isn't any water confronting you, but it becomes more difficult to walk when the mess is right there. Faith is walking and believing while He is still working it out? Sometimes you have to wobble in your walk because it is a little scary to walk by faith. Oh, it is not an easy walk. Don't lie to yourself. It can be a little stressful. Where my folk, where my folk?

When you have to wing it and you don't have anybody else in your life to help you wing it, don't worry. God will help you. He will keep you as you start to walk out in faith. He will keep you until you get over the river. Slap your neighbor a five and say, "Neighbor, just keep on walking till you get through it." I said just keep on walking. Just keep on praising Him. Just keep on giving Him the glory. Just keep on praying. Just keep on fasting. Because as sure as you started, the same God who gave you enough strength to start it, will get you through it!

Joshua positioned himself. They sanctified themselves. They put the presence of God first. Here's the last part. It's in the text. The possession of the promise was on the other side. You must go through the Jordan because going through gives you enough strength to press into your possession and activate your promise. Your promise is across the Jordan. The Jordan is overflowing but when you start to walk, the water backs up. Here's the clincher: the Jordan never overflowed until it was harvest time. It's in the text. The Jordan was overflowing and the Jordan never overflowed unless it was harvest time. So the fact of the matter is it may be rough for me right now, but the real deal is I'm in harvest. Where my folk at, where my folk? I don't have the money, don't have the car, don't have the house, don't have the job, don't have anything, but I believe God for it all. The real deal is it's a mess because I'm in harvest and God wants to give me a greater blessing than this overflow. So you need to slap your neighbor a five and say, "It's mine. I am going further because I am in harvest. I am in harvest. It may not look like a harvest to you, but as sure as I'm walking across this Jordan, as sure as I'm stepping with the Lord, I'm getting ready to walk right into a harvest that eyes have not seen and ears have not heard." I got anybody in here that believes you are in a harvest? I'm right dab smack in the middle of a harvest and I'm going to praise God for my harvest. Let me hear you praise Him!

Everybody standing, I'm finished. I'm going

further than this. I could stay where I am. It's not that it is a bad place, but if I press for the possession on the other side, there is a greater harvest. What gave Israel the courage to keep pressing when they were in Egypt and before they got anywhere near the Jordan River? God made a promise. He said to them, "Everywhere you place the sole of your feet; I'm going to give it to you." It wasn't conditioned upon how they lived. Lord, have mercy! It wasn't conditioned on how much they prayed or praised. It was conditioned on where they walked. If you can step into it and if you can walk on it, it is yours. You cannot be intimidated because the river is overflowing. The river only overflows because of the harvest and harvest means it's your time to receive. So in order to get what God has already stored up for you, you must walk through the overflow.

I've got to coach you and push you. You're too comfortable with this level. Even though it may be a good place, it is not your promised possession. God has more. God has more for you. You haven't reached your apex yet. He has got more. I don't care how good it is, it's not the best He has for you. Are you willing to go further than this? Bow your heads.

Father God, we thank you for being so good. We delight ourselves in your ways because You are good. We spend time telling You how very good You are. But today, Lord, we sense in our spirits that there is more. There is more. We've positioned ourselves on the banks of the river. We're getting ready to step in. We've signified for your presence to go before us. Lift up a standard before us. Help us to keep on walking, pressing toward the mark of our calling in You. We've got to go further because You got some miracles stored up on the other side of this river. We have to push pass this place because You have some blessings on the other side of this Jordan. It is a little scary walking this way, but we will believe to see it. We will believe to see Your goodness. Do it for us because we believe we are going to have what we say. You have the power to make it all right. We must keep walking. You can make every step a step of betterment. Bless us and don't curse us. Make good on what You said. We believe it in Jesus' name.

And just like Joshua took a man out of every tribe, I'm holding on to a sister or a brother's hand. I also believe for them. I don't want to receive by myself. I want some other sisters and brothers to join me in testifying about Your goodness. You are just too big to be good to just me. God, you must be good to somebody else too. Yes Lord, yes Lord. Strengthen the hand that I touch. Cause them to be courageous and strong. Let them know that He who has started this good work in us has many more blessings, and they can go further than this. We bless and we thank You in Jesus' name. Don't clap your hands. Don't clap them. Drop them and then lift them. Let's worship.

Expect It!

And when Jesus was entered into Capernaum, there came unto him a centurion, beseeching him,

6 And saying, Lord, my servant lieth at home sick of the palsy, grievously tormented.

7 And Jesus saith unto him, I will come and heal him.

8 The centurion answered and said, Lord, I am not worthy that thou shouldest come under my roof: but speak the word only, and my servant shall be healed.

9 For I am a man under authority, having soldiers under me: and I say to this man, Go, and he goeth; and to another, Come, and he cometh; and to my servant, Do this, and he doeth it.

10 When Jesus heard it, he marvelled, and said to them that followed, Verily I say unto you, I have not found so great faith, no, not in Israel.

11 And I say unto you, That many shall come from the east and west, and shall sit down with Abraham, and Isaac, and Jacob, in the kingdom of heaven.

12 But the children of the kingdom shall be cast out into outer darkness: there shall be weeping and gnashing of teeth.

13 And Jesus said unto the centurion, Go thy way; and as thou hast believed, so be it done unto thee. And his servant was healed in the selfsame hour.

Matthew 8:5-13

Let's glance again at this story of the soldier and his servant. This particular sermon and its topic were brought to my mind after a phone call I received from

Minister McLean on Saturday. Today's message was fuelled by the voicemail message she left for me regarding her son. I will tell you a little bit about the content of her message a little later. Her son was sentenced to an astronomical amount of jail time and so forth and so on, but we will get to that later. However, something happened which was unbelievable. As I listened to her on the voicemail, I understood absolutely nothing of what she was saying. Somehow she must have realized that because she called right back and left a second voicemail. This time she said, "Co-Pastor, I know you didn't understand me, but let me slow down and tell you what happened." I understood the second voicemail, and you will soon see that all had worked out just fine. After the second voice mail, I began to rejoice about what God had done for her. Then I put together these particular thoughts.

Today, I am going to mess with your theology a little bit. I will do so in order to establish a far deeper fundamental truth in your spirit. I'm going to give you a truth that will help you to keep on believing God when the odds are stacked up against you. So look at your neighbor left or right and repeat my topic after me. Say, "Neighbor, today Co-Pastor is going to talk about *Expect It.*" That's it. That's it. Now look at the neighbor on the other side and say, "Neighbor, today I don't know how much preaching Co-Pastor is going to do, but she's going to talk about *Expect it.*" That is what I'm going to deal with this morning. In just a few moments, I will pass the microphone to Minister McLean. So get yourself ready, Minister McLean.

McLean's story is the basis for my dialogue and discussion with you this morning. Let me begin the dialogue by talking a little bit about faith. McLean did not give up. I am talking about not giving up when everything is stacked up against you. Sometimes we say that things are stacked up against us, but the truth is there is a little opening and if we maneuver just right, get the right lawyer to do the right thing, or write the right resume, we can get the desired result. But sometimes we find ourselves in situations where the odds are totally against us and no one thinks the situation will have a happy ending. However, there is something about expectation that can give your faith some fuel. So this morning I did not come for everyone, but I did come for some brothers and sisters who believe God. Those of you who need a little fuel added to your faith. I came for you. I'm going to help you today. Some of you are not standing right now, you know why? Some of you are just perpetrating. You know you don't have enough faith to get you out of your situation, but rather than tell the truth, you would rather act like you do. Where my folk? Where are the "for real" people? Thank you! I came for you.

I do not have enough time to really dialogue about faith, but I need to talk just a little bit about it before I talk about expectation. There are a few pertinent facts about faith which I need to share with you. Regardless of your position, status or longevity with the Lord, faith is that Christian grace which is constantly being challenged. There go the honest folk. There is something about life and trying to live it as a believer that tests your faith. Where the real folk? Real folk, just waive your hands.

Let me talk about me. I'm going to tell you something that most preachers will not tell you. No matter how hard I try to live holy or how hard I try to do the right thing, life just won't give me a break. I mean if it's not one thing it is another. I am not a weak person and I am not talking about some little bitty thing. Every thing that has ever happened in my life which really challenged my faith has been major. Faith just won't give me a break. Just when I think I have moved into a new arena of trusting God and I can feel my muscles and strength walking in faith, just then, bless God, something happens which knocks me right back to ringside. There I go again trying to conjure up enough of the Word of God to keep on trusting God. Anybody in here going to be real? Slap your neighbor a five and tell your neighbor, "Faith is not easy."

I know all about the "how-to" books. Books like how to believe God, how to get your prayers answered, and so forth and so on. And you know what? None of those how-to books helped my faith. I read them. I highlighted and underlined them. But there is something about believing God and trying to hold on while the situation does not appear to be getting any better. It is difficult. It is difficult to push past some of this stuff in life, especially after you have prayed over it for a while. It is one thing to pray over some stuff for a short time, but it is a whole other thing when you've been praying over some stuff for years. Where my folk? Where my folk?

McLean is coming in a minute. When we first started praying for her son, it would have been a lot easier on our faith if God had worked it out right away. Why is it that faith causes you to face difficulties and keep on believing without a sign of any kind that your prayers were heard? Somebody help me say "change." It is one thing to believe God and hold on during the struggle when there are signs of improvement. All you need is a sign. Just let them sing, "Jesus keep me near the cross." Just any kind of little sign will do! But it is difficult to hold onto God and believe Him when there are no signs that the answer is on the way. Faith becomes tedious when there are no signs. When you trust God to do something or make something come to pass, it is tough. Sure, I can get happy if I see a sign or some sort of change for the better, but it is difficult to keep on believing God without signs of anything changing.

McLean's testimony is one that we should note because she kept her faith even though I know at times it slipped. She is just like you and me. Even though we love God, there are times when our faith is tested. Where the real folk? You come in here jump up and shout and say you believe that the lump in your breast is gone, even though the doctor says it is cancerous. You believe that God is going to heal you, but the first time the doctor says "cancer" to you, you weren't that happy. Don't tell me that when you were in that doctor's office and he announced that you had a lump in your breast and it looked like it may be cancerous, you said, "Thank you." No, it took you a few minutes to recollect. You had to regroup because your momma died of cancer, your grandma died of cancer, and now this man suggests that you have cancer!

It is difficult to operate in faith when we lose expectation. The enemy does not have to get you to doubt God if he can mess with your expectations. Sometimes God cannot do what you ask. Not because He doesn't want to do it, but because you no longer expect Him to do it. Lord, help me. Now Minister McLean is going to come. Minister McLean, when I tell you to stop you've got to stop, but share a little bit of what you expected and how it resulted in a faith move. Sometimes all you need is the expectation and that, in and of itself, can bring about a miraculous change. Come on Minister McLean and share just a little bit.

> *"He [my son] was at the wrong place at the wrong time. Although he was not the initial perpetrator of the crime, he was associated with those that were."*

He didn't do the crime. He was just present with the fellas who committed the crime. This is a good lesson for you young people. They sentenced him just as if he had committed the crime. You've got to keep expecting even when the thing you are expecting doesn't appear to be on the way. Where my folk at? Lord, I hope I don't jump off this stage. I said you got to keep on expecting it even when what you are expecting appears as if you're never going to get it! I'm fueling your faith. You have to keep expecting. Slap your neighbor five and say, "Expect it."

Did you hear what McLean said? She said she started fixing up the boy's room. Her son had been turned down on appeal every time. Every time, no matter what we did, no matter how we prayed, how we fasted, how many letters we sent, how many petitions we signed, they kept on turning the boy down. Do you think McLean's faith was where it is right now? Some days, all she had with her faith was expectation.

We are going to move on, but let me tell you this first. Not only did they overturn the decision, but they have already put the papers in the system for his release. Slap your neighbor a five and tell them, "I expect it to change."

Greater than your faith should be your expectancy! Expect it! Look forward to something that is different. If you look at the text with this Centurion soldier, at first glance you may say that it was the soldier's faith that caused the miraculous healing of his servant. I beg to differ. I do not think it was his faith alone. I'm sure he had some faith because Jesus said He had not seen so greater faith in all of Israel. I'm also sure it had something to do with Jesus' authority to heal. By this time, Jesus' fame had gone out and He was known as the new healer. But deeper than his faith and deeper than Jesus' authority or power to heal, I think this soldier expected something out of the ordinary. I don't know who I came for today, but I came for somebody who has been waiting on something extraordinary. My – my – my! I don't care if you already got the divorce papers. I came for somebody who is waiting on something extraordinary. I'm going to help you today.

If you are not careful, the enemy will distract you from your faith. I repeat . . . if you are not careful the enemy will distract you from your faith. I know all of those faith scriptures. Yes, I know them. "Now faith is the substance... and without faith it is impossible to please him." I know all those faith scriptures, like "the just shall live by faith." I know all of them. But sometimes they don't help me. Nothing is wrong with the scriptures, it's me. I admit it is me. I'm going to be honest. There is nothing wrong with the Word of God. I admit it's me.

47

Because while I'm trying to remember everything in the Word about faith, the situation I'm looking at seems impossible. The enemy does not have to get you to lose faith. He distracts you and messes with your expectation or that part of faith which hinges upon what you expect God to do.

There are three things which the Centurion soldier did not do. He did not allow his present problem to override his expectation. You cannot let what you are dealing with in the present dictate how this thing will turn out. If McLean had allowed the present to dictate her son's future, she would have stopped praying at the first turn down on appeal. I can't get anybody to believe it! When you have an expectation it doesn't matter if the problem was created by you or if you are a victim of circumstance. A problem is a problem is a problem. Lord, have mercy. But what you've got to do is not allow what it looks like in the present to affect what will happen later. You must remember that as long as you can see it better, it can get better.

Let's say it another way and deal with the text. We never read that the soldier gives a whole lot of information about his servant's sickness. Go back and read it. It just says he had a servant who was sick. He was real sick. It does not say how long he had been sick, and the text does not say what caused the illness. No other pertinent information is given other than he had a servant who was sick. The present condition was the man was sick and he needed to be healed. You need to focus on your expectation. I know you have faith and you believe God. I know you trust Him, but let's just take it a little step further. Let's remove the faith and just say "I expect." If you expect it to get better, God can make it better.

According to the text, the Centurion approaches Jesus as if he has a right to be there. Lord, have mercy. Expectation can make you a little cocky. Didn't you hear McLean say she had to cut loose some friends? If you are not expecting what I'm expecting and if you can't see what I see, good bye! This situation requires a miracle, and I need somebody who believes in miracles. Y'all don't want to hear no preaching! I know in the present, things don't look like it will change. McLean and her son appealed to four courts. What would even make them go to another court? What would make them think that if you go to a fifth court, it will get better? Expectation! It is what you expect. Look at your neighbor and say, "I expect!"

You must believe things are going to change even if change is not on the horizon. I'm going to mess with somebody's theology of faith. You have to look forward to it even if your faith says otherwise. What do I mean by that? You have to say things will get better. "That boy is coming out. Somebody is going to do something to let that boy go free." You have to keep on regurgitating what you expect God to complete. I can't get you to believe it but it is true anyhow. Faith says "I believe." Expectation says "I anticipate." You can believe and never anticipate. Lord, have mercy. I said you can believe and never anticipate. McLean was anticipating when she started fixing up the son's room. What good is it for you to believe, if you don't anticipate? If you believe then you have to anticipate that one day this thing is going to manifest itself in the present. You have to say what I'm

49

dealing with now is not the end of my faith. You cannot allow your present problems to mess with your expectation. I know they said they were never going to come to church. That's fine. I anticipate the day they will.

The second thing that this Centurion did not do was let the barrier of distance override his request. Sometimes we do not let the present problem override what we are expecting, but we will let the distance override the request. In other words, because he is in jail, or because he or she is in the emergency ward, or because they are in the critical care unit, or because their heart stopped beating, and they are way over there and you are here, as long as you expect it, there is a reason for a miracle. I don't care if they are in California or Kalamazoo! As long as you expect it, there is reason for a miracle. Slap your neighbor a five and say, "Neighbor, you can't have a miracle because you don't expect it."

I know that the soldier was not concerned with the distance because of what he said. Jesus says, "Okay I'll go to your house." The Centurion says, "No, that's not necessary. He doesn't have to be in your presence for You to lay hands on him and heal him." Jesus does not have to understand everything there is to understand about your situation. Let me say it another way. Because your blessing doesn't seem apparent and because your victory doesn't seem near is no indication that you are not going to get the victory. Do you expect it? Jesus was not in the vicinity of where that sick servant was. He wasn't close by. Yet the soldier believed and expected something would happen. Expectation has nothing to do with what you feel. Expectation has nothing to do with what you see. Expectation lies within your thought pattern and how you hold on to what you're hoping God will do. Where my folk at? Expectation says you'll go to hell and come back just to bless me. Anybody ever had any problems? Anybody ever been in any situations where you felt like all hell was breaking loose and the only thing that you could hold on to was thinking, "Lord, some day, some way, some how, I expect this thing to get better."

Jesus heals the servant, and where the servant was or the circumstance surrounding the servant did not matter. There was expectation. I'm sure McLean had days when she didn't know her left from her right. One phone call from that boy with his heart broken saying, "Momma, I thought you was praying. I can't stay down here. I didn't do nothing wrong." What can you tell a child who is locked behind bars in his early 20's and has 50 something years to go? What can you say to that child about faith? His argument might be "Faith is what got me here. It is because I believed God that the judge and the jury put me here. I mean you said those church folk were praying for me. You said that the Lord was going to hear their prayer. How in the world did I get sentenced in the first place?"

Expectation says no matter how far, how tedious, or how bad it looks, you must keep on keeping on. What expectancy does is it makes you keep coming back. I need to know if I got anybody in Calvary that has made up their mind that they are going to keep on coming back? You may knock me down, you may throw me out, you may tear it up, and you may tell me "no," but I'm going to keep on coming! That is what keeps your faith alive, not that you have the miracle, but you keep on talking about it. You keep on coming back. The soldier did not allow his present problem, the sickness of the servant, override what he was expecting. The soldier did not allow distance to override what he was expecting. He did not think, "The miracle can't happen here, it needs to happen over there." He did not let distance stop him from requesting the healing.

Throw your hands up because sometimes the enemy gets in the air and sends confusion into your atmosphere. Sometimes you have to speak a word to your atmosphere. Let me hear you talk to that devil and say, "Devil, it is not what I think because I don't have any good thoughts about this situation. It's what I say. I say God is getting ready to open up something for me." Say yes! Say yes! Say yes! I didn't come for everybody, but I came for a few folk who need something opened. You have to learn <u>how</u> to <u>say</u> what you expect. I know it's falling down, I know it's breaking up, I know it's busting loose, but I expect something to open up for me. I know they ripped up my application and turned down the loan application, but I'm expecting God to override this whole situation by what I say!

Did you hear McLean? McLean said when the judge said her son was going to do the time, she said, "This boy is coming out." He has been in jail since 1994 and this is 2000 and what? But is he coming out? Slap that neighbor a five and say, "Neighbor, it doesn't matter how long it takes, I expect it to happen." I wish I had a voice up in here. Grab that neighbor by the other hand and shake it real good. Say, "Neighbor, I don't know when it is going to get better, it doesn't look too good right now, but I expect a miracle!"

Watch what you say and watch who is saying stuff for you. Do not hang around with anybody who doesn't believe in the God in you. You must believe that what I believe is coming to pass. You must expect what I'm expecting. I am not expecting that boy to be a senior citizen in jail, but I expect him to get out and walk out and say, "To God be the glory!" You have got to watch what you say and do not be intimidated by what somebody else says. I said watch what you say and don't let anybody intimidate you by what they say. McLean was not intimated by the fact that the first court said no. Second appeals court, no. Third appeals court – some years later -- said no. The fourth appeals court said they were going to agree with the other three courts. But you cannot be intimidated by what somebody else says. You have to lift your expectation to a higher level. If I have to eat hot dogs and pork and beans for forty days and nights, I am still expecting. Slap that neighbor on the shoulder and say, "Neighbor, do not be crippled in your expectation by other folk." Don't be crippled in your expectation by other folk, but learn how to say the right thing.

You have to learn how to say, "When there is no way being made, I expect a way." The Lord will make a way. He knows the way that I take and when this trial is through, I'll come forth as pure gold. You have to say what you expect. The battle is not mine. If the battle is not mine then who does the battle belong to? The battle belongs to the Lord. The race is not given to the swift and the battle not given to the strong, but if I can endure and hold on, God will work it out for me. You have to expect and say what you believe. I believe that eyes have not seen and ears have not heard what God is going to do for me. I believe that what I'm expecting God to do will blow my mind. Grab that neighbor's hand for the next to the last time and shake that hand like you're going to shake it off, and say, "Neighbor, you've got to talk the right talk." Grab the neighbor's hand on the other side and pull on it real good. Say "Neighbor, you've got to talk the right kind of talk. You've got to say the right thing."

Let me tell you something that will blow your faith right through the ground. The miracle that was wrought with this Centurion and his soldier was not wrought just to be miraculous. Let me suggest to you that the miracle which took place was not healing. The miracle which took place in that soldier was expectation. I said the miracle wasn't that the servant was healed. The miracle was not in the healing. The miracle took place by what the soldier was expecting. Let me qualify it. Jesus says to the soldier, *"I have not seen so great a faith in all of Israel. Go home and whatever you want will be there when you get there."* He did not say I'm going heal him. He said go home and whatever you want will be there when you get there. The miracle did not take place in the healing. The miracle took place because the soldier expected God to do it.

Listen to the conclusion. You can walk expectation right into a miracle. The soldier walks home expecting the servant to be healed. Look at your neighbor and tell them, "I'm going to walk into something here." I am going to walk into something today. I'm going to walk into something up in here today! Lord, have mercy. When the Centurion arrived home, they told him the servant was healed and the Centurion said, "Okay. When did it happen?" I said you can walk into something. It may not show up until October, but you can walk in it today. When did the fever break? The same hour! Luke, Matthew and John say that the servant was healed the same day. Now, I don't know how long it took the soldier to get home, but what I do know is that the man got healed the same hour Jesus told him to go home. If you can expect it today, Jesus will work it out tomorrow. Grab your neighbor's hand for the last time and say, "Neighbor, oh neighbor, I expect a miracle and I expect it to happen today." I may not get it till tomorrow. I may not receive it until December 31, but I expect it today. The self same hour that you expect God to do it, God will. God will! Where my folk at? God will do what you expect Him to do. Turn around and high five three people and say, "I'm expecting a miracle! I'm expecting the miraculous. I'm holding onto a victory. I believe God for another anointing. I'm trusting God for a better time. I'm holding on for a better day. I'm walking in a better miracle. I believe. No! I expect it! I expect a miracle! I expect the victory. I expect it. It's on the way. It's on the way. It's on the way!"

I came for somebody to tell you to *Expect It*. I know the loan company said "no" and turned you down, but go to another loan company and fill out another application. I know they said that you don't qualify, but go to another supervisor and fill out an application. Is there anybody in here that is just like that soldier? I don't know when God will do it, but I expect it. If I expect it, it will show up. Tell me how it's going to change. Tell me when it is going to get better. I expect it. Yes I do. What I like about the soldier is that he not only had the right kind of talk, but he had good expectation. Listen to his question.

He didn't ask anybody how long the servant had been well. He didn't say, "Tell me, did you start getting better little by little?" He asked one question. "When did it get right for you?" That tells me that from the time Jesus said go home, until he got there, he expected things to be better. That is my last group. From the time you leave here until it gets better, I want you to expect something better. I don't know when you are going to get it and I don't know how long it will take, but expect it. When I get mine, I'm going to tell you about it. When I get it, I'm going to testify that same day. I will dance for it. The same hour that I expect it I will dance about it. The hour I expected it, that is the day and the hour that the Lord did it! Is there anybody in the house today that can dance on expectancy? I don't have it. I don't know when I'm going to get it. It may be a long time coming, but today I will praise God because I expect it!

I told you that expectancy means anticipation. Anticipation means I will stand back and wait. Expectation means anticipation and anticipation means I just . . . I just wait. If folks ask, what are you doing? Just tell them "I'm waiting." No matter how many folks ask you and how many times they ask, "What are you doing?" You tell them, "I'm waiting." What are you waiting for? "I'm looking forward to a change. I'm waiting for them to get saved. I'm waiting for a financial breakthrough. I'm just waiting." How long are you going to wait? "However long it takes." It may be four years, four appeal courts, and four different judges, but I will wait for however long it takes. I expect it. I wish I had a voice because God knows I can't preach this like I feel it. I'm going to be honest with you. I have waited on this one for a little bit of time and my faith was shot, but today, I feel a revival in my expectation. I'm going to dance right here for what I expect is going to happen because God is going to make it happen for me. I expect it!

Throw your hands up. You might as well clear your air – just clear the atmosphere. Tell the devil, "I admit you messed with my faith and I have had a hard time trying to believe God for my breakthrough, but today, I am not going to worry about no faith. I want you to know that I expect it to change!" I preached this word this morning, but McLean wasn't here. A little sister came up crying and said "You never know what this sermon has meant to me." She said her son had just been sentenced to 135 years. I didn't ask her what the boy did. It is none of my business. But she said, "Today I expect a change." You have to expect it. Your faith may get a little fuzzy but keep your anticipation high.

The point of the Centurion story was not the miraculous healing of the servant; it was the fact that the Centurion soldier expected it. Sometimes the miracle is not in the manifestation of what you trust God to do. The greater miracle is that you expected it all the time. Slip your hand in somebody's hand. I don't know who I'm here for today. But just like that mother at 8:00 service, whose faith was a tattered because 135 years is unbelievable in anybody's book, God fueled her faith with expectation. He can fuel yours too. It is not that we believe, it is that we believe with anticipation. There are plenty of people who believe, but do not anticipate. Lord, have mercy. They have faith without expectation. But just like McLean, you must believe and you must anticipate that no matter how it looks in the present, expectation says a change is on the way.

Close your eyes, bow your heads and hold on to that hand tightly. Father, we come to You honestly and sincerely, not trying to act like we have the right amount of faith--even though a small amount would be enough. Sometimes the present problems outweigh our faith, but we're coming today asking You to help us. Just like that Centurion soldier was saying, if You just speak something, the whole thing would get better. Just like the Centurion soldier, we expect the miraculous. Help us to say the right thing even when we don't feel the right thing. Help us to speak the right thing even when we don't see the right thing. You don't have to rearrange everything. You can change it right here. You can give the victory right here. Just like the soldier had to walk back home to see the full manifestation of what You spoke to him, give us as believers enough expectation to keep on walking until we, too, see the full manifestation of what You spoke.

I'm holding on to a brother or a sisters' hand. I'm not going to ask you, Father, to give them more faith. I'm going to ask You to give them expectation. The hand that I now touch, help them to expect something new. Help them to expect something better. Help them to expect a victory. Help them to expect a way out. Help them to expect a way being made and, when they have received the full manifestation of what You have spoken, help them to testify that it was that self same hour that they praised You with expectation. It was the day that I found joy in my expectation that God manifested the fullness of the blessing. We thank You for it now in Jesus' name. Just keep those hands extended. Extend those hands. Keep your eyes closed, your heads bowed, and those hands lifted up. Expect the miraculous. Expect the extraordinary. Expect the impossible.

Move Your Hand, Lord

And he said, My presence shall go with thee, and I will give thee rest.

15 And he said unto him, If thy presence go not with me, carry us not up hence.

16 For wherein shall it be known here that I and thy people have found grace in thy sight? is it not in that thou goest with us? so shall we be separated, I and thy people, from all the people that are upon the face of the earth.

17 And the LORD said unto Moses, I will do this thing also that thou hast spoken: for thou hast found grace in my sight, and I know thee by name.

18 And he said, I beseech thee, shew me thy glory.

19 And he said, I will make all my goodness pass before thee, and I will proclaim the name of the LORD before thee; and will be gracious to whom I will be gracious, and will shew mercy on whom I will shew mercy.

20 And he said, Thou canst not see my face: for there shall no man see me, and live.

21 And the LORD said, Behold, there is a place by me, and thou shalt stand upon a rock:

22 And it shall come to pass, while my glory passeth by, that I will put thee in a clift of the rock, and will cover thee with my hand while I pass by:

23 And I will take away mine hand, and thou shalt see my back parts: but my face shall not be seen.

Exodus 33:14-23

Let's go to the Word of the Lord in the Book of Exodus. Glance over at your neighbor and repeat my subject after me. Say, "Neighbor, today Co-Pastor is going to talk about 'Move your hand Lord.'" Look at the neighbor on the other side and say it just like me. Say, "Neighbor, oh neighbor, today Co-Pastor is going to talk about *'Move your hand, Lord.'*" Let the devil hear you say it. Throw your hands up and signify and say, "Satan, today is my day for the Lord to move His hand!" Say yes! Move your hand Lord.

To understand the dialogue that is really taking place in our text between Moses and God it is necessary to provide a brief analysis of a previous conversation between God and Moses. Certainly, I don't have time to divulge all of what happened in the previous conversation, but if we are going to understand the setting for this text, we must at least look at part of the previous conversation between God and Moses. In God's previous conversation with Moses, God gave instructions to Moses and the children of Israel to whom Moses had been given charge.

One of the fundamental laws and rules which God gave to Moses was the instruction that the nation of Israel could never, ever, have any other gods above the invisible God. God was very clear in this dialogue and discussion with Moses. God said that as Israel migrated through the wilderness and into the promise land of Canaan there was one cardinal law which would never be tolerated by God. Israel should never erect statues of gold or silver and call them god and should never ever – never ever --erect any idols or any images and say that they were god. Even though the surrounding nations and culture may have had gods of gold and silver, Israel as a people and as a nation would never ever do anything that would allow any other imagery to surpass their invisible God. Never would Israel have gods made of any idol or any other kind of idolatry or imagery.

Moses then tells the people of Israel that they can never erect statues, shrines, temples or idols and worship them as god. Israel understood what God had said before going into the land of the Canaanites. They knew it coming out of Egypt and they knew it as they came out of bondage. No gods but their invisible God. Upon their deliverance out of Egypt, while Moses is on Mt. Sinai having the second conversation with God, the nation of Israel made some ill-conceived decisions. They decided to erect a statue-- an idol--and worship the idol and call it god. They made this decision because they thought Moses was taking just a tad bit too long up on that mountaintop. They thought maybe God was not paying attention to them. So they took off their jewelry and melted down ornaments and erected a golden calf.

The golden calf imagery was the power symbol of Pharaoh. For them to erect a golden calf and dance and celebrate it as if it was the power of a Pharaoh in Egypt that t delivered them was an insult to God. Can you imagine how God felt? While God is having a conversation with Moses, while God is giving Moses additional information and instruction, the very people God has sworn to bless is down at the foot of the mountain rejoicing and worshiping and celebrating an idol that they have erected with their own hands, calling it god. Can you imagine how God must have felt?

Well, let's not be too hard on the nation of Israel because there are some folk sitting among us today who are guilty of some of the same kinds of behavior. Oh, no, no, no, you don't have little statues sitting in your living room or little imagery sitting in your kitchen, but you are guilty of the same behavior. For you have gods called cars. You have gods called houses. You have gods called bank accounts and money market accounts. You have gods called job positions. You even have family gods and friend gods. You got all kinds of idols that you have erected and you celebrate them instead of celebrating the God that gives you life. Let me mess with you just a little bit this morning before we get heavy into it. Never worship the blessing more than you worship the Blesser. I will help somebody up in here. I said never worship the blessing more than you worship the one who provided the blessing for you. Don't get stuck up on where you live, or what you drive, or your annual income. Don't get hung up on that. You get hung up on the God who gave you the strength to do, to receive and to have!

Moses leaves the top of the mountain in utter disgust after he learns that God's instructions were already being ignored at the bottom of the mountain. These same people who God had brought out of Egyptian slavery had lost their minds. They are at the foot of the mountain having some type of celebration with a golden calf. They are dancing, jumping, shouting and screaming that it is the calf that brought them out of bondage. Moses is so disgusted with their behavior that in his frustration he drops, or throws down, the tablets of stone.

That brings us back to our text. Moses' only recourse now that the tablets have been broken is to go back and say something else to God. He returns to the top of the mountain to resume his conversation with God. As he begins the conversation anew with God, he says to

God, "Okay, God, you have every right to be angry with my people. They have certainly proven themselves an ungrateful lot. They have broken the cardinal rule, Lord." Nevertheless, Moses says to God, "If You get rid of them [Israel], You have to get rid of me first." It's in the text. Take your time and read it in your leisure. Moses says to God, if you destroy the nation of Israel, you must destroy me first.

Now, some of you aren't bothered by what Moses said, but if you are like me, I began to wonder. What kind of relationship did Moses have with God that he could talk to God with that kind of language? I mean can you get the gist of this conversation? Here is a mortal human being talking to the God of the universe. If You are going to mess with my folk, You will have to come by me. What kind of a relationship did Moses have with God to even suggest that he could put his life on the line for somebody else?

This question brings up a point of scrutiny. It is not one of my main points, but certainly a point you need to pay attention to. Some experiences that you have in life, especially some bad unpleasant experiences, are not the design of the enemy. I'm going to mess with somebody's theology, because you thought everything good came from God and everything bad came from the devil. I'm going to mess with your theology. Some of the unpleasant situations and experiences that you're dealing with have been designed by the hand of God so that He can enhance your walk with Him. Who am I talking to up in here today? Some of us would never move to the next level in God unless God caused some bad things to happen in our life. Oh, you don't want to hear any talk today. God can't let only good happen to some of us because we would never experience the mighty hand of God. He must turn our world upside down, make us cry a little bit and make us want a little bit because if He kept giving us good things, we would never seek Him like we're suppose to seek Him.

Everything bad that happens in your life has not been wrought of the devil! Some of this stuff God has ordered! He has ordered it because it's the only way He can lift you up to a higher calling. Well, let's say it another way since you believe that the steps of a good man are ordered by God. Tell your neighbor say, "Neighbor, fit with it and don't fight it." Look at the neighbor on the other side and say, "Neighbor, fit yourself with it and don't fight it." There are people who are trying to fight the design of the Lord. What God wants you to do is fit yourself with it. Don't fight it because in the end, though the vision tarry, it shall surely come to pass. God is not trying to hurt you, but if He doesn't let some hurtful experience happen to you, you'll never seek Him the more. God will turn your world upside down and make you pray a little more and make you fast a little more. He'll let something that you never expected to happen happen. You will find yourself saying, Lord I never knew this. I never knew they would walk out. He'll let something that you never expected, something that you couldn't imagine in a thousand years, happen. He'll let it happen just to get your attention. If we believe He knows everything and that He is omniscient in His knowledge, that nothing is hidden from Him and that He knows the end at the beginning, then we've got to know that God knew that they were going to build a calf. It certainly wasn't a surprise to God. So if God knew it, then God had a reason to allow it to happen. Slap your neighbor five and say, "Neighbor, God has a reason for this. It's a mess right now, but God has a reason."

God wanted to show Moses that the children of Israel had a long way to go in their love and loyalty to Him. He wasn't trying to hurt Moses and make Moses feel bad, but He was trying to show Moses that everybody on the row didn't love God the way he loved God. Everybody in the pulpit doesn't love God the way I love God. Everybody on the deacon board doesn't love God the way you do. Everybody in the choir doesn't love God the way you love God. I am not scared of anybody up in here! You got people in the missionary department and part of the prayer band that don't love God the way you love God. People are here today for all kinds of reasons. Everybody didn't come in here with a clean heart and holiness on their mind. Somebody came up in here cruising. I said I ain't scared of anybody up in here! Some of you came in here because your momma told you to come.

So God will let some bad things happen so you might understand that everybody that says they love God, don't really love God. Some people only serve God for what they feel God will give them. The moment God stops blessing them, they stop serving Him. God was really trying to help Moses out. Check out who you hang around with. Everybody who is smiling in your face doesn't like you. Some people just want to get your secret. They just want to find out where your weakness is,

67

especially if they came out of the same stuff you came out of. You better watch folk who came out of the same stuff. If you've been delivered from being a whoremonger and fornicator and committing adultery, don't hook up with somebody that came out of the same kind of stuff. Get yourself somebody who has come out of something different so they can keep pulling you up! Why would you hang around with folk that are just like you used to be? Lord, have mercy. You didn't do anything but drink liquor and smoke blunts, and you come right into church and find the very one who is still drinking liquor and smoking blunts. Get yourself together. God is trying to show you something.

God wasn't trying to hurt Moses. There comes a time in every Christian's life when you need to figure out where you are going. If you're not going where I'm going, then we will have to say it was good while it lasted, but I have to go! Somebody better help me right here. You crazy to give up all you gave up outside of the church and then come in the church and let somebody mess you up. I don't think so! If I gave up everything I gave up outside of the church and God saves my soul, I will not let some half stepping, no good, play Christian mess me up. Honey, call me stuck up, call me a holy roller, or call me sanctimonious, but get out of my way. I can mess up by my self! I don't need you to pull me down.

God was trying to teach Moses. All those folk came up out Egypt, and they didn't all come out with the right motives. God wasn't trying to hurt the Israelites. He was trying to show them and show Moses that He could take what seemingly is painful to you and cause your pain to be a gift to another person. Who am I talking to? God can take what's hurting you and bless somebody else. If you're taking notes, this is a good little something to note. Somewhere between now and then, Jesus will cause you to feel some pain you can't explain. Lord, have mercy. I don't know who I'm talking to, but I know I'm talking to somebody besides me. There have been some painful situations in my life that I honestly cannot explain. I didn't know if it was the devil. I didn't know if it was God. I didn't know if it was a generational curse or if I ate it, drank it, or fast it up. I didn't know if it was the anointing. All I know is because of the pain, God gave me enough grace to testify.

That is what is wrong with some of you. You won't talk about your pain. You are trying to live in some type of fun-fantasy world, like every day with Jesus is just wonderful and you never hurt or go through anything. You just get up in the morning and call those things that be not as though they are, and God just answers all your prayers. Liar! You are struggling just like me. You barely made it in here today, and if God didn't help you, you would make a fool out of yourself tomorrow! Where my folk at up in here? God has the unique ability to take your embarrassment and turn that thing around, so that when He gets through with it, what the enemy meant for evil, God makes it good.

Moses is hurt by the fact that his people went back on their word and built this golden calf. He is hurt by it. God takes what is hurting Moses and He uses it. He uses that hurt to give Moses a bargaining tool to intercede for the same people who are hurting him. Who am I talking to up in here? You're hurting. It is unpleasant. It looks bad, but no one knows that God is getting ready to use you to intercede for them. That's why everybody in your family is not in a mental institution. That's why everybody on the job is not cussing and fussing. God is using what's hurting you. That's why when you look back over your life, you can say, "If it had not been for the Lord who was on my side. . ." That is the reason why I got a testimony. Not only did somebody pray for me, but honey, I prayed for someone. I prayed for them when they were cursing me! I prayed for them when they were laughing at me! I prayed for them when they were talking about me! God will use your pain as a tool for intercession. Slap that neighbor on the shoulder and say, "Pray for me."

I know you are hurting, but if you are hurting, then you're in the best position to pray for me. I know you're embarrassed because your own daughter made a fool out of you, but pray for me. The people who understand pain can labor in prayer. Don't pray for me if you haven't been through anything! If I'm starving, I don't want anybody putting their hands on me who has never been hungry a day in their life. I don't want you trying to encourage me and you have never had a discouraging situation yourself. What are you going to say to me? I need somebody who has, at the very least, walked where I'm trying to walk. The Bible says that through Moses' pain, he gained the ability to intercede for the people. The hand of God designed what he was experiencing.

Why did God design it? Good question. God is not like us. He doesn't do stuff just to be doing stuff. You know us. We just do stuff to be doing it. Sometimes, we don't even know why we're doing it. We just say it because we're big enough to say it. We just do stuff just to be doing it. Most times, we don't have a reason for doing what we do. If we had thought about it, we wouldn't have done it. The fact is we did it without thinking about it. We do stuff without any reason, but God is not like that. If God does something, God has a reason for doing it. He allowed the pain so that Moses could become an intercessor for the people.

So God had a higher reason for allowing Moses' pain. First, God wanted Moses to seek His presence. Let's stop there a minute. There are too many of you in Calvary today who are just trying to seek God's face. "Lord, I just want to seek His face. I want to get up in the face of God. Where is the face? Lord, the face, the face, the face, the face. I've got to get to the face of God." Let me tell you something. You are never going to get to His face. All those prophets and people you listen to on the televangelist circuit that say they've been up in the face of God are lying. I'm going to show you in just a minute where God tells Moses that no body can see His face and live. Oh, I'm going to help somebody up in here! Give them this tape for me. There are too many of you up in here trying to get to God's face. What you need to be seeking is His presence. Slap that neighbor five and tell them, "Seek the presence of God." Learn not to go anywhere, do anything, say anything, or be with anybody that does not have the presence of God. That's why some of you are in trouble right now. You are hanging out with the wrong group. You're hanging out with the group who is trying to get to the face of God so they can get blessed, but they never reach the presence of God where they can feel the anointing that comes with one who walks close

71

with God.

God wanted Moses in a place where he would seek His presence. I admit that our journey with God is a faith journey. In a faith journey, you need to seek God's presence. I also admit that sometimes on our journey with God, we cannot feel His presence. But for those of you who know that you know, that you know, that you're walking in the presence of God, it doesn't matter whether you feel Him or not. It's all in what you know. God was trying to bring Moses into a deeper revelation of who He was. Moses knew God, but he only knew Him through the face-to-face burning bush experience. He talked with the bush and the bush talked back. It burned, but it was not consumed. But now God brings Him up the mountain. There is no burning bush. If Moses is going to talk to God, he has to believe that He is without seeing Him, without feeling Him, without any new car, and without any additional blessing. He must believe to see, and he must see that God is alive that He is a rewarder of them that diligently seek Him. Who am I talking to? God is trying to move you into a position where you seek His presence. Slap that neighbor on the other side a five and say, "Neighbor, oh neighbor, this next level that God is trying to bring you to will take you into His presence. I'm not talking to everybody, but I got some folk in Calvary today who have made up their minds that whatever it's going take, whatever I have to do, I must get to a place where I am in His presence.

So Moses is up on the mountain top in the very presence of God and he is having a conversation and a discussion with God. In the next verse, God says to Moses, "Come on up into another place." I've come for somebody in Calvary today who has been wondering, "What will it take for me to reach the next level?" Once you are in the presence of God, God himself will call you up into a new place. Listen to the scripture. God said to Moses, come on up to this next place. He says it like this, "Come stand next to me on this rock." Psalm 16:11, says it like this, "God show me your path and your place." In the path and the place where His presence is there is fullness of joy. At His right hand, there are pleasures forever more. I don't know who I'm talking to, but if I'm talking right, there is a place in God where your sadness can become joy.

Therein lies my second point. There is a place in God where your pain can bring happiness. There is a place in God where the abuse you experience can give you glory. I don't know who I'm talking to, but I'm talking to somebody today that's been going through. You've been lied on, been cheated, been talked about, and mistreated, but it brought you to a new place. It brought you to a happy place, and now you can count it all joy. Slap your neighbor five and say, "Neighbor, get in a place where you can call it joy." It may not feel like joy, but you can get in a place where you can call it joy. It may not taste like joy, but you can get in a place and call it joy anyway. It may not feel like joy, but you can get in a place and say, I will bless the Lord at all times! His praise shall continually be in my mouth. I dare you to jump up. Let the devil see you. Count it joy. Joy in the morning. Joy in the noonday. Joy when they walked out. Joy when they came in. Joy when they talked about you. Joy when they laughed at you. I can dance today because I called it joy. Joy! Joy! Joy!

You must get to a place where you call it joy. You must get to a place where you look at what the devil is trying to do, and you call it joy anyway. David called it "gain, a secret place." He said that they who abide under the shadow of the Almighty, can get in a place where you hunger and thirst after righteousness. You can get in a place where being with God is more important than a Mercedes Benz. You can get in a place where having communion with God is better than the five room house with a bathroom in every bedroom. You can get in a place where you have communion with God and every day with Jesus is sweeter than the day before. Shake that neighbor's hand say, "Go to a place. Go! Go!"

Moses was in a place where he was seeking God's presence. When he got to the place where he was seeking His presence, God put him in a new place. When he gets to the new place, he starts propositioning God. Yes, he does. It is in verse 18. Moses says to God, "Show me Your glory." It's the same in both translations. Can you imagine being in such a place with God that you can proposition Him? God says to Moses, "What?" Moses says, "I'm in the place, I'm standing up here on this rock, I sense Your presence, now here is my proposition. Show me!" I got anybody in the room that wants to get to the place where you can proposition God? Where my folk at, where my folk? I don't mean proposition Him for houses and land because if you get to the right place, you don't have to worry about houses and land. Why? Because God said He would give you the desires of your heart, if your ways please Him and you walk uprightly.

Moses propositions God saying "Show me your glory." In this context the word "glory," means show me "your weight." In other words, Moses says, "I want to know how heavy you are. You say you are better than Allah. You say you are better than Sweet Daddy Grace and the Honorable Mohammed. Show me your heaviness. Show me your weight. Show me your worth. You say you can do what no other God can do. Show me what you are made out of. Show me if serving you is worth everything I've given."

This leads me to my third point. It's your time to push God. It's your time to set God up. It's your day to push God. Where my folk at? I dare you to jump up, clap your hands, and praise God with a push. Praise Him. Push it up! Push it up! God says to Moses, "You are pushing me, but I cannot show you My glory. If I show you My glory you will die, but since you pushed me, and since you are in the right place, what I will show you is My goodness." It's in the scripture. I cannot show you the glory, but I can show you my goodness. When God talks about His goodness, He is not talking about a blessing. When God talks about His goodness, He is not talking about just any old thing. When God talks about His goodness, it is synonymous with God's favor.

So God said to Moses, I will not show you My glory but I will show you favor. That is why when you filled out that loan application and God knows you do not qualify, the loan officer says, "I don't know why I'm doing this, but I feel like you're good for this one. I'm going to let you have the loan." That is why when you walked into the BMW dealership and God knew you didn't qualify for a BMW or Lexus, you got one anyway. Why? Because the Bible says when God shows you favor, there is no devil in hell that can stop God's favor on your life. So you didn't qualify for the BMW and everybody thought you were making a fool out of yourself, but you went into the dealership anyway because favor is just favor. I said favor is just favor! You don't have to like me, but if I have favor! So you walk into the BMW dealership. You say, "I don't want a 2002 because, it's almost September. Where are your 2003's?" You don't even qualify for a 2000, but because of favor, when you leave the dealership, you're driving that car. Somebody say, "Drive it – drive it – drive it!" I dare you to jump three times for favor! Favor! Say yes! God said He cannot show you glory but He can show you favor. He can take you to a place where there's nothing but favor.

So Moses is working with favor. Lean on your neighbor and say, "That's what I'm working with. I'm working with favor." I am not working with my bank account, I'm working with favor. I am not working with the right recommendation, I'm working with favor. Say, "Favor!" The Bible says Moses was working with favor. He was in the right place. He propositions God. If You have to give it to anybody, give it to me. I've got to have the favor.

Here is my fourth point. In verse 22, God tells Moses that he is in the right place, but He has to put him in the cliff of the rock because "My goodness would take you out of here if I do not cover you with my hand. You have my presence. You are in the right place. You have propositioned me with the right kind of question. You are pushing me to do something. So I will protect you with my own hand." That is the next to the last group I came for today. You thought that it was all over, but God sent me here to tell you that He has you covered. The enemy can't do but so much because God has covered you. He is protecting you with His own hand.

Let me help you to understand what I'm saying. You may get sick, but you won't die because God has a covering over your life. You may be broke, but you will come up again because God has a covering over your life. I may be down, but keep an eye on me. I'll be back again because God has a covering over my life. He has a protection over my life. He has a protection over my marriage. He has a protection over my home. He has a protection over my kids. He has a protection over my money. He has a covering! I need somebody to jump up and praise God because God is covering, covering, covering. Grab your neighbor by the hand and shake it like you're going to shake it off. Say, "Neighbor, ask me how I know I'm covered." Then tell them, "I'm covered because according to His word, my covering is goodness and mercy shall follow me." I'm covered! I'm covered from the crown of my head to the soles of my feet. I'm covered! I'm covered from the rising of the sun till the going down of the same. Slap three people a five and holler, "Covered!"

Moses is in His presence. He is moved to a new place. He propositions God with the right kind of request. He pushes God to move His hand and protect him. But then, something happens in verse 23 that messed with my theology. How in the world, in verse 22, do you take your hand and protect me, but then in verse 23, you remove your hand and expose me. Something is wrong! Because if you have my best interest at heart and your goodness is your favor, why would you protect me and then move your hand, Lord? To understand verse 23, you must continue reading Chapter 34.

Let me help you. He covers Moses in verse 22 then, in verse 23, He removes His hand, but keep reading because the conversation continues. Now instead of Moses doing the talking, God picks up the conversation in chapter 34. God says to Moses, "I'm glad you finally arrived and because you're in the right place with my presence around you and you did not proposition Me for houses and land, I'm going to make you a promise." So in chapter 34, God makes Moses a promise, but He does not leave the promise to Moses' imagination. He says to Moses, "I will remove my hand so you can see the promise." In verse 11, God names the promise. He says, "… and when I make a promise, here's what's going to happen." Chapter 34, verse 11 says, "I will destroy the Canaanites." He calls them by name. "I'll destroy the Amenities. I'll destroy the Hittites. I'll destroy the Perizzites." In other words, Moses, you are going to live to see the promise fulfilled.

Moses died before they entered into the promise land, but you must understand that when God gives you a promise about a wealthy place, it goes from everlasting to everlasting. I came to tell my last group of folk that God is getting ready to remove His hand because this promise is not going to stop with your generation. This promise is going to go to your kids and your grandkids. Help me out, David. Yeah, I'll help you out Owens, I've been young, and now I am old, but I have never seen the righteous forsaken or His seed begging bread. God made you a promise. He is not a man that He should lie. He is not the son of man that He needs to repent. You can do like Moses, you can praise Him because God is good for it. If God promised it I know He is good for it. Does anybody in Calvary have a promise from God? Have you already been protected, already been in His presence, already moved up in a new place, and already asked for the right kind of proposition? All you have to do now is wait for the promise to be manifested.

I have some enemies all around me, just like Moses, but I believe to see the goodness of the Lord in the land of the living. All I have to do now is thank God for moving His hand. Move your hand, Lord. Move your hand, Lord. If You move your hand, You will make my enemies my foot stool. If You move your hand, You will prepare a table and anoint my head in the presence of my enemies. If You move your hand, eyes have not seen and ears have not heard what you have prepared for me. I need somebody to jump up, let the devil hear you say it. Move your hand Lord! Move your hand, Lord! Move your hand, Lord! Move it, Lord! Move it over my marriage. Move it over my money. Move it over my health. Move it over my kids. Move your hand. I have a promise. God is getting ready to do something for me. I don't know who I'm talking to, but I'm going to give you 10 seconds to praise God for the movement of His hand.

Wait a minute, I hear the Holy Ghost. Slap your neighbor on the shoulder and say, "I can praise Him for the movement of His hand because in God's hand there is power, power, power, wonder working power. I'm like Moses, I don't know what is going to happen when I leave this mountain, but what I like about God is that He will set it up so that what I lost in the beginning will be doubled at the end. Let me prove my point. When Moses started this conversation, he didn't have anything in his hand. He had dropped the tablets and they had broken, but keep on reading chapter 34. He walks back down from God's presence, out of the new place with the right proposition, and had been protected with goodness and mercy. He had a promise, but guess what? He had some new tablets in his hand! What the devil stole had been replaced!

God is getting ready to move His hand and put it back in your hand. Can you praise Him for the promise? I have power in my hand. I have praise in my hand. I have prosperity in my hand. My God! Throw your hands up and say, "Move your hand, Lord!" Say "Move your hand, Lord." Hallelujah. Move your hand Lord. Do what you do best. Bless me, Lord, with the movement of your hand.

Who would have thought that the same fumbling Moses would have received power in his hand from God? Power! Power! Power! So much power was in Moses' hand that God asked him, "What's in your hand?" Use what's in your hand.

Dear God, our father, we stand in your awesome presence trying to get to a place where we are beside You. Call us higher, Lord, higher in You. Call us to a place where faithfulness outweighs prosperity. And whether we are prosperous or not, we are content being in a place with You. Thank you for the right kind of talk so that we proposition You right. We know that if we ask for the godly things, You will give us the good things. We know that if we live a godly life, You will fill our life with goodness and favor. Thank You for presence that brings us to a place of the right kind of proposition, Lord God, the kind of proposition that pushes You to do something -- something good for us. Thank You for the push that we can give You to protect us. Cover us with Your hand. Allow Your hand of covering to be all around us. Don't just cover us, but cover everything that concerns us. God, your hand is big enough and it is weighty enough to cover everything. We commit to Your hand. Cover us, Lord, protect us in Jesus name.

Then God, we have promises. Move Your hand so we can see the full manifestation of everything You promised. Every enemy that rises up and every tongue that lifts itself up, bring it down. Don't let the enemy triumph over us. We believe in the promises of God. We are the head and not the tail. We are the first and not the last. We are who You say we are. We are priests, a holy people, a peculiar people, and a holy nation. Show forth Your praises. Thank you for promises, and then thank you, Lord, for equipping our hands just like You did Moses. Put something in our hands, something we can possess and bless with. Something we can give. Something we can pronounce upon those who are close to us. Just like we are holding hands in this room today. Bless our hands that we may bless the hands we touch. Thank you for my sister or brother who is standing next to me now. With these hands of power, I pronounce a blessing. Bless their going in and their coming out. Bless them in the city and bless them in the field. Bless them when they are going and bless them when they are coming. Let the promises that they have received be manifest before the year is out. I prophesy over this hand. I prophesy a blessing in this hand before the year is out. Now Father, we say thanks and give You praise. Drop those hands. Hold your clapping. Drop those hands and lift them in worship.

In the Meantime

35   Cast not away therefore your confidence, which hath great recompence of reward.
36   For ye have need of patience, that, after ye have done the will of God, ye might receive the promise.

Hebrews 10:35-36

Come on and put those hands together if you love Jesus. Come on and clap like you love Him. Some trust in horses and some trust in chariots. God knows I will trust in the name of the Lord for the name of the Lord is a strong tower. Let's say "Amen" for the Word of the Lord. Amen. I am preaching for me today. This one is for Co-Pastor Susie Owens. Bless His wonderful name.

Look at your neighbor left or right and repeat my subject after me. Say, "Neighbor, *In the Meantime*." Look at the neighbor on the other side and say it just like me. Say, "Neighbor, oh neighbor, today Co-Pastor is going to preach about '*In the Meantime*.'" Now clap your hands and take your seats.

Let me begin my discussion today by saying to you that the real character and substance of faith is perseverance. I know there are all kinds of theological definitions and scholarly reaffirmations to define faith; however, if we could reduce faith to its lowest common denominator, faith's real essence is the ability to keep on keeping on. It is the stamina to keep on keeping on, to persevere, to be persistent and not give up. Faith then is the catalyst that gives us substantial footage when life's turmoil comes. You know life is full of turmoil.

Perseverance is that element of faith that is able to keep us going on. In the midst of life's ups and downs, faith's answer to life's struggles is to strengthen you with might so that you can go on. In the midst of problems that have no real solutions there are decisions that have all kinds of consequences. There are some decisions with consequences that have no final answer. It's just one thing after another, after another, with no final end to the chaos going on in your life.

I am talking to believers. It is our faith that continues to push us forward. Faith is like a log rolling contest. It may best be described as a log rolling contest. Let me explain because at least 90% of you here today are not familiar with a log rolling contest. In a log rolling contest, the contestants must display precision. They must have an inward and innate tenacity to endure. In a log rolling contest, one's agility must be at its best. As the contest begins, two opponents take their positions on a section of a 10-to-12 foot long log. They position themselves on top of the log. This is not easy to do. It is not easy to substantiate your footage in the middle of a log that is moving under your feet. Not only must the participants stabilize and station themselves on top of this 10-to-12 foot-long log, but the goal of the contest is simply to stay on top. Contestants must stay on top of the log while their opponents (the enemy) try to make them lose their balance and fall off.

This scenario is similar to life and life's situations. In order for you to maintain your footage, you must be quick with your footwork and quick with your reactions. Your decisions must be made immediately and you must never tire of balancing yourself. If you lose your balance, you will surely fall off the log. The enemy acts the same way when you're trying to deal with life. Yes, I know I didn't come for everyone, but surely I came for some other folk beside myself. The enemy will cause you to lose your balance while you are trying to stay on top of life's situations. It is the enemy who moves the pace of the log along. You respond by shifting yourself and moving from left to right in order to stay on top. The danger is you can get dizzy. I didn't come for everybody, but I came for a few folk in here who are trying to balance life without getting too dizzy, as things can happen so quickly. Sometimes, things happen so fast that you barely have time to react to one thing before you have to react to something else. If you're not careful, the struggle to stay on top can cause dizziness. I know some folk don't want to tell the truth, but I don't mind telling the truth. Sometimes, I get a little confused because things are happening so quickly around me. It is not a matter of my believing God. That is not in question. It's just that life doesn't always line up with what I believe. I can't get anybody to help me, but that's okay. Sometimes life just doesn't line up with what I believe. I believe it is going to happen, but I have nothing in my life to suggest it is going to happen.

When you are on top of that log, you don't have a team mate. You don't have anybody to pass the baton to. You don't have anybody who can set up a dribble, so you can get it in the basket, and there is nobody looking for you to throw you the football. You are on top of that log all by yourself. You must maintain your footing without getting dizzy. If you want to win, you must learn how to steady yourself and go on. You must learn to go on. You must develop the ability to stay on top of the log, even in the midst of fast moving water currents. You must visualize it. Here you are trying to balance yourself on top of this log in the middle of the moving water and you have an opponent who is working on your last nerve while you are trying to stay on top. I'm going to help you today. Sometimes, life resembles that kind of a contest. Sometimes, that is how we are as believers. We often must shift our faith, so we can keep on moving.

The enemy will create a certain amount of pressure in the waters of your life. Unexpected movements can enter your life and cause you to take your focus off of God. If you want to keep yourself balanced on top of that log, you must know that within yourself lies the ability to keep on going! You must ask, "God, help me to keep on keeping on." You must develop patience and endurance to be able to balance and believe what God has spoken to you in the midst of trying situations. You must believe what God has said. I may not have anything on top of the log to substantiate my claim, but I know what I know. I see the waves, but I know and believe that if God spoke it, then somehow, some way, I will survive this situation and not fall off the log. We must, as believers, develop a philosophy that will allow us the ability to stay on top.

Now I know everybody does not have the same kind of testimony. Some of you handle things so nice and easy. You don't ever doubt God. You don't ever wonder why it is happening to you. Everything that happens in your life, you readily accept it as the will of God, and you don't have any pressure. Well, God bless you. Hallelujah to the lamb! The rest of us are sick and tired of struggling without any results. Some of us are trying to hang on in there while our hands still have blisters from what we just came through. Some of us are still wiping sweat and tears from our eyes so we can balance getting up the next morning.

The text says do not throw away your confidence and your trust in God. Do not throw away your confidence, when God takes too long to answer prayer. Do not throw away your confidence, when God takes too long to change your circumstance. Do not throw away your confidence, when God takes too long to rescue you out of that situation. Do not throw away your confidence, when God takes too long to heal you. Do not throw away your confidence, when God takes too long to deliver you. Sometimes, it is not the balancing of the log, but it is the <u>time</u> it takes for God to do something. Now I know everybody in here can't talk to God like this, but sometimes, God just gets on my last nerve, and I am not being sacrilegious either because me and God have a wonderful relationship. So you stay out of my business and mind your own. But sometimes, I can talk to God and tell God He is on my last nerve. It is not even a matter of holding on. It is not a matter of holding out, or a matter of giving up. Sometimes, God just takes too long. I just say to Him, "God, you taking too long!" I need somebody in here who can agree with me that sometimes God just takes too long. It seems like He is just taking His sweet old time. It appears as though He is not paying attention to what I'm going through.

It is not that I doubt God. I know He has the ability. I know He is all powerful. I know God is God and there is no other God beside Him. I know He is El Shadai. He is Jehovah Jireh and Jehovah everybody else, but sometimes He just takes too long! I am not talking about praying one prayer. I am not talking about one time of fasting. I'm not even talking about one time of calling those things that are not as though they were. I'm talking about **time**, honey. I have put some time into this situation. I have believed God when I didn't have anything in me to believe Him for. I have held on to God when I didn't have anything to hold on for. I have danced, skipped, shouted, wore my clothes out, sweated out my hair, and He has not moved yet. Sometimes, God takes too long!

I want to be honest today. I am tired of this kind of struggle. I am tired of trying to balance myself. I am tired of trying to stay on top of this log. I have stood in the mirror and talked to myself. I have looked right foolish. I have said, "You are embarrassing me, God." I am passed frustrated. I am now embarrassed. Everybody on the job knows my story. Everybody in the family knows my story. Everybody on the block knows my story, and You have not moved yet. God, you are taking too long! I know some of you are too holy to be truthful, but how many of you have been embarrassed by God? He has plain old embarrassed me! He had me calling Him a deliverer and nobody is delivered yet. He said He was going to save them. I could balance myself a little better on top of this log if, at least, they were coming to church! I repeat, "You said You were going to save them. It would be easier for me to balance myself on this log, if You would just move on their heart and let them come to church! It's been five years and they have not come to church yet! I am embarrassed!" I came to tell you don't throw away your confidence in God, even when He is taking too long.

Now you must understand that the writer of the Book of Hebrews, the Apostle Paul, was not writing to sinners. This particular text was not written for unbelievers or non-Christians, but the writer of the Hebrews text is writing to believers. This letter is written to sanctified, blood-washed Christians who were in need of some encouragement. My assignment today is to speak into the lives of some believers in the Nation who need a little bit of encouragement. This message is going to work for you and it is going to work for me.

Before I get to my points, one way to encourage a believer and fortify a believer's trust and confidence in God is to remind that believer that no matter what trial, temptation, persecution, tribulation, distress or famine they are facing, you've had other trials before. So when you try to fortify a believer's courage, you must get them to look back on their past victories. Since the time you first started this journey with God, until your present day situation, you should have had some struggles. When you made it over your trouble, you should have stopped and built a memorial.

You remember when the children of Israel crossed over the Jordan into the Canaan land? They stopped and took 12 stones and built a memorial. Each stone represented a tribe and they would call the memorial Ebenezer. Ebenezer means "the Lord helped us." You need to go back in your past history and realize that God helped you when you were facing other trials. You should have built an Ebenezer, a memorial, so that as you try to balance yourself on top of the log, in the middle of your situation, you would know that God will help you because God helped you before. I have some Ebenezers in my life. I have some Ebenezers that nobody else at 610 Rhode Island Avenue has. As sure as I am at this microphone, I have some Ebenezers, and I told the enemy that the Lord will help me through. The same God who helped me deal with that hitherto will help me now. I would have fallen off this log a long time ago. I would have made a complete mess and fool out of my life, but hitherto the Lord helped me. Say, "Help me!"

It is a little shaky right now and the waters are a little deep right here. The currents and the waves are beating against my log, but hitherto! Hitherto, my foot is planted. Hitherto have the Lord helped me. There comes a time in a believer's life when you must encourage yourself. There are times when you must stand your own ground and let every devil demon out of hell know you will not fall off your log. I'm not going back, and I will make it one way or the other. I'm going to endure the trial. I'm going to stand the test, and I will make it through this. This is not the first time I've been through, and this is not the last time I will go through. This is not the first time I've been hurt and it surely won't be the last time. It is not the first time I've been broke and it ain't the last time I'll be broke. In the meantime, I am going to steady myself.

Paul says, "Do not throw away your confidence." Cast not away your confidence in God. My first point is if you are going to keep your confidence level up, you have to believe that God is with you. Now say to yourself, "God is with me." God is with me! In the midst of whatever you're dealing with, in the midst of whatever you believe God for, in the midst of whatever is going right and whatever is going wrong, you must believe that God is with you. You cannot rely on your mother. You cannot rely on your daddy, your husband, your wife, or your prayer partner. There comes a time when you have to look in the mirror while balancing life's struggles. You have to tell yourself "God is with me."

Let me make it a little clearer. Some people like Biblical examples. In the Book of Acts, Paul left for a journey (according to Acts around the 27th Chapter), he and some colleagues and some soldiers were going to Rome. They boarded a ship and set sail. The sea was calm. The captain announced on the loud speaker, "Ladies and gentlemen, this will be a smooth journey. The winds are on our side and the waves are working in our favor. It will be an easy journey. We're getting ready to cast off." The horn sounded. Everybody was relaxed and anticipated a nice cruise. Everything was working in their favor. Paul was down in the bottom of the ship. There was no need to be disturbed or aggravated. Every thing was working all right.

I know there are some folks here who can attest to that. I know I can. When I started this journey, I had smooth waters. Every thing was working in my favor. Folk were speaking well of me, telling me how good it was that I had changed my life and abandoned some of my poor habits. They thought I was on my way to a nice time with God and that this was just the beginning of my life. Just buckle up now and relax because God is on your side. "No problem," I thought to myself. "The rest of my life has got to be better than it was." I started with Jesus and had all kinds of expectations and anticipation. Life was honky, donkey dory. But just like Paul, I had a big surprise.

Paul and the others were on the ship midway in the sea. They had gone too far to turn around. They had to keep going. Midway the sea, out of nowhere according to the text, a storm arose. Not just a mediocre storm either; it was more like a tidal wave. The waves were so high and the wind was so strong that it began to beat upon the boat. The Bible indicates that, little by little, the boat was falling to pieces. The captain and the crew panicked. They had the lives of these travelers and the cargo in their hands. So they started rustling and throwing cargo overboard. Have you ever felt like that while trying to balance life's struggles? You start throwing stuff over board. You ponder over who you need to get rid of --- him or her. You think, "I need to get out of this mess. I need to get off of this boat." I came for somebody in here today. You wonder, "Maybe I need to let go of this person and maybe I need to pray and fast more. What's wrong with my life that I can't seem to get it together?"

The Bible says that while the captain and crew and the others are going through all kinds of antics, Paul got up and made an announcement. He said, "Here ye men and brethren, fret not yourself, the angel of the Lord spoke to me last night and said not a life will be lost." You must believe that God is with you. God is with me. Sometimes, I cannot feel Him. Sometimes I cannot see Him. Sometimes I don't understand what He is doing, but I have chosen to believe that God is with me. The ship may go down. The ship may be torn up. But when it's all over, I will be balancing on top of the log. You must believe in the midst of everything that God is with you.

It does not matter if it is morning, noon time, or the midnight hour, God promised to be with you. Your momma may leave and your poppa may leave, but He will never forsake you. He will not leave you. While you're struggling, He will be right there. You must believe Him and keep your courage up. Keep believing. Do not lose your courage. The same God, who started it, will finish it. It is not over until God says it is over. You may have to cry and you may have to walk by yourself, but keep your courage up. The Lord will make a way some how. The Lord will get me out of this mess because the Lord delivered me out of that other mess. Since the Lord got me out of that mess, He is the same God yesterday, today and forever and He will get me out of *this* mess. I need to hear some praise. Somebody praise Him. Give Him the glory right here. Slap three people a five and tell them, "Keep your courage up! In the meantime, keep your courage up!"

The text continues. Don't throw away your confidence in God. It will be richly rewarded. I'm going to stay with these two versus. In other words, if you don't throw away your trust in God, God is going to give you something in exchange for it. In order for God to exchange and barter with you, you must have something to exchange and barter with. What you have is your confidence, your trust in God.

My second point is if you keep your confidence in God up, He will richly reward you. He will give you what you ask of Him. I knew I wouldn't get too many of you happy there, but I'm going to help you. Some of us are so reserved. We don't want to catch ourselves in a tizzy. So we hesitate to say He will give us what we ask for, just in case we don't get it. I'm going to help you too.

In the Book of II Kings, there is a story about Elijah and Elisha. I'm telling you if you keep your trust in God, He will give you what you ask. He is going to exchange with you and give you what you ask of Him. The Bible records what Elijah said to Elisha. He said, "Man of God, today the Lord is going to take me. This is my day of departure. My departure is at hand. God has already told me that this is my day to relieve myself from this earthly pilgrimage and go on to be with the Lord." He says to Elisha, "Stay here at Gilgal." Elisha says to Elijah, "I'm not going to stay here at Gilgal. Wherever you go, I'm going." I took the liberty of looking up Gilgal for you. Gilgal means the place of circle. Have you ever been in a situation where it seems that you keep going around in circles? You think you got over, but you look around and say, "My God, I've been here before. My God, is that the same thing I was dealing with last year? Why is it that it seems like I'm just going around in circles? I try to pull myself up. I try to balance on top of the log. I try to tell myself it is going to get better, but every time I blink and open my eyes, I'm in the same spot I was in before. I saw this problem before. I dealt with this temptation before. I dealt with this trial before. All I'm doing is going around in a circle, but I'm going to believe as I go that one of these days the Lord is going to help me."

The Bible says Elijah and Elisha left Gilgal and came to Bethel. Elijah tells Elisha, "Stay here at Bethel." Bethel means the house of our God. Elisha says "No sir,

I'm going where you go." Do I have some folk in here who didn't feel like coming to church this morning? It was all you could do to put your clothes on and get yourself together? You didn't care what your hair looked like, bad hair day . . . no hair day. You didn't care about your makeup. It took every ounce of strength you had to make it to the house of God, but I'm glad you're here, because the devil didn't want you to get here. But God brought you once again to Bethel, to the house of God. And since you're here, God says He is going to richly reward you. He is going to give you what you need to make it through the year. He is going to speak to your heart today like He has never spoken before. He is going to hook up to your little faith and stretch your trust, and before it is over, you are going to say, I was glad when they said unto me let us go into the house of the Lord. The presence of the Lord was there. Where his presence is there is fullness of joy. Slap that neighbor on the shoulder say, "I'm glad to see you're here." You made it through all the craziness. You made it the through all the madness. The devil didn't want you to get here, but God gave you enough strength to make it to Bethel and God will reward you.

They left Gilgal and made it to Bethel. They left the place of the circle and made it to the house of God. When they left Bethel, they came to Jericho. Somebody say "Jericho." Jericho is called the city of the palm tree. It is where vegetation grows. It has good fertilization. It is where things that were dead can be made alive. I've got some folk in here who are just like Elijah and Elisha. Life was pressing me too. It was beating me up. My faith was almost dead. My confidence level was slipping, but I thank

God I made it to Jericho. I'm at a place of new life. I had a rough week. I had a rough month. God knows it has been a rough year. It has been all I can do to hang in there, but I finally made it to Jericho. I'm at a place where I can live and not die. Lean on that neighbor and say, "Neighbor, you don't know who you are sitting beside. It's a good thing you sat beside me today because I'm in a place where you can find life. I'm in a place of new life. I'm in a place where I can grow. I'm in a place where I can let go and let God."

They left Jericho and the Bible says Elijah said to Elisha, "Stay here." They came to Jordan –it's in the book -- and when they got to Jordan, Elijah said to Elisha, "You have been following me all day long. You stayed with me at Gilgal. You left and came to Bethel. We made it through Jericho, and I'm getting ready now to cross over to Jordan." When you look up Jordan it means the place of crossing where one can cross from death to life, where one can cross from goodness to goodness. He says to Elisha, "Stay here." Elisha says, "I'm only going to stay if you stay." Elijah looked at Elisha and said, "Man of God, what do you want?" The Bible says Elisha looked at Elijah and said, "Give me a double portion of your anointing." I told you God will give you just what you ask Him for. The Bible said Elijah scratched his head and said, "Man of God that is a hard thing. It is not my anointing to give to you, but if you wait with me, when the Lord crosses me over, if you can stay and hang in there until God gives me a deliverance, then what you ask for God will give you." Now grab your neighbor by the hand, shake that hand like you are going to shake it off and say, "Neighbor, did you hear what she said? God is getting ready to give me what I asked for!"

The Bible says Elisha had to blink his eyes. He had to wipe away the tears because his friend was getting ready to go, but he had to steady himself and stay on top of the log. The Bible says a chariot of fire was released out of glory. Elisha didn't let the fire blind him. Elisha didn't let the hard stuff keep him back, but he kept his eyes focused on Elijah. Elijah said goodbye. Elisha was hollering "Give me what I asked for! Give me what I ask for! Give me what I asked for!" The Bible says Elijah turned around and threw off his mantel. The man of God ran and picked it up and said thank you for giving me what I asked for. I need some folk in Calvary today who believe that God is going to give you what you asked for and that He is going to exchange with you because you believe Him. All I know is that I believe God. I need some folk in the Nation to throw your hands up and tell God, "Give me -- give me -- give it to me -- give it to me -- give me what I ask for!" Let the devil here you say, "Yes! Yes! Yes!" If you keep your courage up and believe that God is with you, He is going to exchange for your confidence and He is going to richly reward your faith.

Verse 36 says you need the power to persevere. You need the power to be persistent. You must know in whom you have believed, that you have done the will of God, that you have continued steadily in spite of the difficulties, that you have persisted in spite of the obstacles, and that you have kept your mind and your heart focused on the things of God. I told myself this week that I had come too far not to last now. I have to go on. I have to last. I can't fall off. I can't lose my footage. I can't give it up. I don't care what the devil is doing. I made up my mind it won't break me. I must last. Lean on somebody and tell them, "I have to last too. I have to do it. I must last."

My third point is what is going to give you the ability to go on and what is going to give you the stamina to stay with God when the log is slipping under your feet. It is going to help you balance life so you stay on top of the log. Point three is you must learn that whatever you're going through, thank God for it. You must thank God for it. You must thank God over it. You must thank God in spite of it. You must give Him the glory when the tears are streaming out of your eyes. You must praise and call it good when nothing good is happening. That kind of thanksgiving is a form of praise. Look at your neighbor and say, "It's a form of praise." When you start thanking God for everything, when you start praising God in everything, you open up some possibilities. Say "possibilities." When you praise God in the midst of your trouble, when you give Him thanks for everything you are going through, you open up some possibilities. Point your finger at somebody and say, "Neighbor, I'm getting ready to praise God for possibilities."

Let me see if I can give you a Biblical example. In II Chronicles around Chapter 20, it relates the story of Jehoshaphat. Jehoshaphat was the King of Judah. You know Judah. Praising Judah was the praise team. The Bible says Judah was surrounded by the enemy. The Bible says the enemy of Israel had surrounded them and other nations had joined the pact. They had made a deal. They said, "We can't kill Israel and Judah one by one, but together we can. Let's surround them." The Bible says

Jehoshaphat looked on the hillside. There were enemies with chariots and soldiers with weapons surrounding Judah, but Jehoshaphat remembered the Word of the Lord. The Word said, "The battle is not ours. The battle belongs to God." So Jehoshaphat says to himself, "I better get some praise in here so I can open up some possibilities." The Bible says Jehoshaphat called for the Levites to get him some singers. He called for the praise dancers. The enemy had drawn their swords and mounted their chariots, but the Bible says that Jehoshaphat gave the order to the Levites to praise God and sing onto the Lord a new song.

The Bible says that the Levites began to sing and the dancers began to dance. They praised Jehovah. They gave God thanks for His goodness and mercy. They praised Him for being their Jehovah Jireh -- the Lord that is always present. The Bible says the more they praised, the more they gave God glory. The Lord God inhabits the praises of His people. While Judah was praising God, the Bible says that God released a band of angels and sent an ambush for the enemy. He gave Judah a breakthrough and a break out. He surrounded their enemies. I need to know if I got anybody in Calvary today that has made up their mind; in the meantime, I'm going to praise Him. In the meantime, I will call Him good? I'm going to praise Him for a breakthrough that has some possibility. I don't know when. I don't know where. I don't know who, but in the meantime, I'm going to give God a praise that will birth a possibility. I'm going to give Him a dance that will birth a possibility. I'm going to shout. I'm going to scream. I'm going to clap. I'm going to jump a praise that will give me a possibility. Open up your mouth, clap your hands and praise Him for possibilities.

Wait a minute because some of you still didn't get it. Let me make it a little clearer. You must give Him thanks. You must give Him praise when it doesn't fit your circumstance. You must give Him the glory. You got to scream and shout when it doesn't fit your circumstance. Now open up your mouth, clap you hands, and give God a praise for possibility! Praise Him because when you praise Him, God will release some of His promises. It's in the book. When you give God the glory, He will give you what He promised. He promised that weeping may endure for a night, but joy is coming in the morning. He promised that many are the afflictions of the righteous, but the Lord delivers him out of them all.

I'm trying to get through, but just look at anybody, it doesn't matter who, just look at anybody and say, "Neighbor, I don't have too much strength because I've been trying to stay on top of the log. So my strength is getting a little week, my foot almost slipped, but today my confidence is rising." I believe to see the goodness of the Lord in the land of the living.

I want the devil to know my foot was slipping and I was close to losing my footage, but today my confidence is rising up. Say, "Neighbor, I want that devil to hear me say I will bless the Lord at all times." In the meantime, I don't know when it will get better. That's not my problem. I just have to stay on top of the log. I don't know when things will change. That's not my concern. I just have to solidify my footage so I don't fall off. God is with me. He is with me. It is a bit of a journey, but He will give me just what I asked Him for. I can't worry about how. I can't concern myself with my opponent. I must thank Him for it. He knows the way that I take when I can't explain it to anybody else. All I can do is praise Him for the possibility. He will not disappoint me. He will hold me up when I want to sit down on the log. He will strengthen me against the enemy. My God will hold me up. He will not allow the enemy to triumph over me. It is my day to encourage myself as well as you. Hold on girl, hold on. Hold on, my brother. I know the log is moving fast. Sometimes it feels as if you're steering against the currents but hang in there. Just give Him thanks for it. God knows how much you can take. Just stay on top of the log. In the midst of all the madness and craziness, sometimes you can't even think straight, but God will hold you in the hollow of His hand.

Lord, give us a spirit of peace because our strength is in Your peace. Oh God, we can handle it better if we have some peace. We could shut our mouths, if we had some peace. We could take our hands off of it, if we had some peace. Send a spirit of peace in this house . . . Holy Ghost peace . . . sweet peace. Peace in our minds. Peace in our hearts. Peace in our spirits. Peace in our mouths. Peace in our hands. Peace in our feet. Give us peace! Thank you for peace today. Send peace to my sister. Send a spirit of peace to my brother. I appoint peace -- peace over the home. Peace over the job. Peace in the family. Peace in the finances. Peace in the body. Peace! Send peace so I can sleep tonight. Send peace! Peace over the kids. Send peace. We command a spirit of peace. In Jesus name, we speak peace to it now. In the meantime, give us peace. Drop those hands. Don't clap them. Lift them and worship. Come on, lift Him and worship. Peace.

Working with God's Plan

1   Then Jerubbaal, who is Gideon, and all the people that were with him, rose up early, and pitched beside the well of Harod: so that the host of the Midianites were on the north side of them, by the hill of Moreh, in the valley.

2   And the LORD said unto Gideon, The people that are with thee are too many for me to give the Midianites into their hands, lest Israel vaunt themselves against me, saying, Mine own hand hath saved me.

3   Now therefore go to, proclaim in the ears of the people, saying, Whosoever is fearful and afraid, let him return and depart early from mount Gilead. And there returned of the people twenty and two thousand; and there remained ten thousand.

4   And the LORD said unto Gideon, The people are yet too many; bring them down unto the water, and I will try them for thee there: and it shall be, that of whom I say unto thee, This shall go with thee, the same shall go with thee; and of whomsoever I say unto thee, This shall not go with thee, the same shall not go.

5   So he brought down the people unto the water: and the LORD said unto Gideon, Every one that lappeth of the water with his tongue, as a dog lappeth, him shalt thou set by himself; likewise every one that boweth down upon his knees to drink.

6   And the number of them that lapped, putting their hand to their mouth, were three hundred men: but all the rest of the people bowed down upon their knees to drink water.

7   And the LORD said unto Gideon, By the three hundred men that lapped will I save you, and deliver the Midianites into thine hand: and let all the other people go every man unto his place.

8 So the people took victuals in their hand, and their trumpets: and he sent all the rest of Israel every man unto his tent, and retained those three hundred men: and the host of Midian was beneath him in the valley.

9 And it came to pass the same night, that the LORD said unto him, Arise, get thee down unto the host; for I have delivered it into thine hand.

Judges 7:1-9

God is talking to Gideon. God tells Gideon to go down to the valley where the Midianites are camped. "Arise, Gideon. Get up and go down to the place where the Midianites are for I have delivered them into thine hands." Look at your neighbor, left or right, and repeat my subject. Say, "Neighbor, oh neighbor, Work with God's Plan." Look at the neighbor on the other side and say, "Neighbor, I need to ask you a question. Are you working with God's plan?" That is what we are going to talk about today, *Working with God's Plan.*

I am going to take a few minutes to talk about providence. Let me be clear before I go any further. I am not going to suggest that you do not have control over what you do. Because sometimes when you talk about providence, people take the ideology that they have no control. Some folks believe that whatever happens just happens. They say "God is going to work it out. I am not responsible." You are wrong! You must assume responsibility for your choices. God does have providence, but He will not work against your will. So you are responsible for whatever it is you are doing. Now that we have that straight, let's talk a little bit about providence.

When I talk about God's providence, I suggest to you that God has a plan. God has a plan to move His creation to a certain end. God has plans to bring all of creation to a predetermined end. In other words, God has a goal and an aim for His creation. He has predetermined the way this whole thing is going to end. He started it all -- in the beginning was God -- and He is going to end it. When all of this is over, there will be God and the end that God has already predetermined. When we talk about the providence of God, we are talking about the process. There is a planned process which God has already designed to cause this world to end. What will happen in the end? By God's design, in the end all He has created will worship Him. God plans to end this thing like He began it, with all of creation worshipping Him.

I believe that God has highly exalted Him and given Him a name above every name and that at the name of Jesus, every knee will bow. I did not come for everybody. I came for one group and I am going to talk to that one group for the next few moments. Those folks are the ones talking back to me right now. I believe that every knee is going to bow and every tongue is going to confess that Jesus Christ is Lord. When this whole thing is brought to an end, every created thing will worship God, the father.

With that in mind, I am almost through with my talk on providence. So let's define providence as God's ability to order events. God can cause certain things to happen. He can devise a plan, call it divine, and make certain things happen. God can lead this whole creation into His predetermined end. In other words, God has a purpose for everything that happens. God is not like us. God doesn't just do stuff! Sometimes, we just do stuff to be doing it. But everything God does, He does for a specific reason. He has a reason for everything He does.

Now, I admit that God does not always include us or tell us what He is doing or why, but there is always a reason. God has his own particular method of doing what He does and His reasons for doing it. Well, let's say it another way. God has intentions. He has intent. Some of the stuff that you are going through is intentional. He did not put the stuff there to hurt you. He put it there because God has intention. If we do not establish the fact that God has a plan, that He does not always disclose the plan, and that His plan may not fit with our plans, we will have problems. As sure as I am on the microphone today, I know that there is some stuff in your life which God did not discuss with you and you had to deal with it. You don't have a clue about how long you will have to deal with it either. You don't have a clue about who God is going to use to get you out of your current stuff. But hear me, some of the stuff in your life was intentionally put there by God.

Working with God's plan is not always easy. It is not easy because God's thoughts are not our thoughts and God's ways are not our ways. God has a divine reason for doing what He does and a divine goal. Now this is a good spot for you to witness to your neighbor and say, "Neighbor, if you are going to get along with God and work according to God's plan, you will have to want what God wants." Help me, Jesus! I need a little help. Where my group at? My group, stand up! I didn't come for every body. That's right. I want y'all with me the whole sermon.

If you aren't standing now, don't you stand later on. This is my group. This is the group I came for today. All right, sit down my group. I just wanted to know where you are. Thank you, Jesus.

You have to want what God wants. I did not say you have to like it. I said you have to WANT it! I don't always like what I have to go through. I don't always like what is happening to me, but I've decided to work with the plan. I'm going to help my group. I am not helping anybody but my group. The rest of you can take a nap! I'm helping my folk. What God wants you to understand is that He has battle strategies that you haven't even dreamed of. God has a way of doing things that will blow your natural mind. God has a way of doing things that will make you think you are going crazy. God will put you through some stuff and when you look back on it, you will think you are the one who is off. But it is all part of the plan. While you are sitting there thinking, "This thing can't work," God is thinking "It can!"

Let's return to the text. God says to Gideon. Get ready to fight the Midianites. No problem. Now according to historical background, when God tells Gideon to get ready to fight the Midianites, the Midianites have already assembled themselves down in the valley next to the Israelites. When you read it in the commentaries, it says there were so many Midianites that you couldn't count their camels. No problem. God said go fight. Gideon goes through all of the tribes trying to muster up some fighting soldiers. Meanwhile, the Midianites encamped and covered the scope of the valley as far as Gideon could see. All Gideon sees is the enemy. He goes through all the tribes trying to get some soldiers. When he counts the fighting soldiers on his side, he comes up with 32,000. Now some people might say that was a good number of troops, but no, that was not good because the Midianites had triple that number. However, if you make up your mind from the beginning that you are going to work according to God's plan, you'll be just fine.

When you are working according to God's plan, you must understand that God can get you out of any situation despite how insignificant you may think you are. You don't have to have good credit in order for God to give you a new car. You don't have to have good credit for God to get you out of your mess. If God has a plan to get you out, you can have bad credit for 10 years, but when it's your time then it's your time!

Gideon had 32,000 soldiers. He goes back to God and says, "Okay we are getting ready to fight." However, he felt like his 32,000 was no match for the Midianites. "Lord, I'm getting ready to fight" even though he felt he could not handle it. "Okay, I'm getting ready to fight," even though he felt some pressure because 32,000 was nothing compared to the fighting men in the Midianites' camp. But listen, while you are thinking you can't, God knows that you can. When you are thinking it is over, God knows it is just beginning. When you are thinking that it is too little, God says it is too much because He has a plan.

Gideon says, "Okay God, I'm ready to fight." Gods says "Wait a minute, hold up. You can fight, but Gideon, you have too many men." Now put yourself in Gideon's place. Can you hear him saying, "What do you mean? Prophesy to me!" God tells Gideon he has too many men. God tells him, "I cannot work my plan with all these men." God tells Gideon to reduce the size of his army and that the reduction will take place in two stages. Now can you imagine what Gideon is feeling and thinking? "What do you mean I have too many men? You want to reduce the army? What do you have in mind?" God tells Gideon that the first reduction of his army will result by asking one simple question. God told Gideon to tell all the soldiers who really did not want to fight to go home. Some of you don't understand the significance of that question. Gideon says, "Okay, I've got 32,000. Anybody who doesn't really want to fight, you are now relieved of active duty." 22,000 soldiers walked out! Where my folk? Where my folk! I came to tell my folk that if you work with the plan, God will work it out even after your supporters and your friends walk out. Help me say, "Yes!" 22,000 resigned!

My first point is if you are going to walk and work according to God's plan, you will have to pass some life's test. When God uses life to test you, it will cause some separation. His plan calls for isolation. Somebody will desert you. Lord, I feel you in this place. It is not about you, it is about the plan. The 22,000 could not have stayed if they wanted to because God has to separate. When life seems so unkind, when life causes you to feel unappreciated, and when life causes people to be ungrateful, life will make you cry. Where my folk? I don't care how long you been saved. I don't care about your prayer life or what kind of anointing you have on you. When you mess with life, life will cause you to cry! Sometimes, life is just overwhelming. Is there anybody in here who will tell the truth? Sometimes, it's just a little bit too much. When you are in the middle of a life's test, the only thing you can do is cope. You can't change anything. You do not have the power to rearrange anything. You just have to cope with it! You have to look at life and make up your mind, "I didn't expect it to end like this. I didn't expect it to turn out like this. But I will not die with it."

When you cope with life's situations and when you are being tested in life, you must be poised. You must have a certain amount of confidence which says "I can handle this, one way or the other. I'm coming through this one way or the other." You must have a certain amount of confidence and a certain amount of assurance that if God started this plan, then He has the power to end it. Slap somebody a high five and say, "God will work it out!" Where my folk, where my folk?! I came to tell my folks to keep your composure. Keep it up! Keep it up! Whatever you are in the middle of, keep your composure! God is testing you. It is a life's test.

Now, 22,000 had already resigned. God tells Gideon that He still had a plan, but Gideon still had too many men. Gideon must have thought, "Too many? Hey Lord, have you seen the enemy? What about the enemy?" But God says, "I have a plan. Take your army down to the river." I told you God will make you think you are going crazy! Here Gideon was getting ready to fight all these folk and God was talking about the river. What does water have to do with anything? Slap your neighbor five and say, "Work with the plan. Work with it!" God does not have to give you an explanation! Just work with it! Gideon goes down to the river with the 10,000 soldiers who are left. In the back of his mind, he hears God saying "too many men." Then God says He is going to put the 10,000, in a water-drinking contest! And there are NO rules! All God wanted Gideon to do was stand back and watch. Where my folk?! Do I have anybody here who has ever had God put you in a contest and not tell you the rules? You just have to stand there and take it? God told Gideon to take the army down to the river and tell them to drink the water.

Ten thousand men start to drink. Some of them drink nice. They scoop it up and focus on the water, but then there was another bunch who knew that when you get in trouble, you cannot focus on one thing, you must drink and look around. You just have to lap it up, honey. You don't have time to be scooping up anything. God asks Gideon how the men drank. Gideon says "I have a whole lot over here who are drinking right." God asks about the other group. Gideon says, "The other group? They are just radical. They are just lapping it." God then tells Gideon to dismiss the majority bunch and take what was left. The Bible says when Gideon looked again and reduced the army, he was left with 300. I need somebody to signify to your neighbor and say, "Neighbor, whatever you do, stay with God." Clap you hands and let me here you praise Him right here.

The Bible says that when the contest was over Gideon was left with 300 men. That was all he had left to fight. Here comes the second test. Not only will life test you when you work with God's plan, but God has a way of giving you a spiritual test. Look at somebody and say "spiritual." Now when God gives you a spiritual test that means God places a divine situation in your life and you must rely on the Word of the Lord to sustain you. Some of the things you have been going through have you wondering if it is really of God? God sent me here to tell you that He is giving you a spiritual test because He wants to know how much of his Word do you have in you. And let me tell my folks this, being spiritual does not mean you drive a Mercedes or a BMW. Being spiritual does not mean you have $100,000.00 locked up in a bank account somewhere. Spirituality does not equate to prosperity. We have this thing backwards. You can be spiritual and ride on the metro. You can be spiritual and live in an efficiency apartment. Spirituality is based on how much of the Word you have in you. Slap somebody a five and say, "I believe in the Word, I believe in the Word and I have the Word locked up inside of me."

God gives Gideon a spiritual test to find out how much of the Word is locked up in Gideon. If you are going to work according to God's plan, you must know what you know. When you feel like giving it up, when you feel like letting it go, when you feel like turning it loose, you must have enough of the Word in you to know that "He that hath begun a good work in me must complete it." I can't let it go. I can't turn it loose. I must keep pushing. I have to keep holding. I have the Word locked up inside of me. When it looks like it will not get any better or when my strength feels like it is about to fail, I have enough Word in me to know that God is a present help in the time of need. I got the Word. I got the Word! When the enemy rushes in like a flood, I got the Word. I got it! I got it! Say yes!

God gives Gideon a spiritual test and He says to Gideon "You have 300 men. Divide the 300, into three companies of a hundred. Put one hundred on the left, 100 on the right and 100 to work it in the middle." I agree with Bishop, sometimes you can't go to the left or to the right. Sometimes you just have to work it in the middle. In the middle of the mess, you must keep on working the plan. In the middle of the trouble, you have to work it in the middle. Where my folk at -- where my folk? Grab your neighbor by the hand and shake that hand like you are going to shake it off and say, "Neighbor, just work it--just work it -- just work it right where you are." The place where you are, even if it is the middle, is a place of purpose. Say, "Purpose."

Now when God brings you to a place of purpose it means God has brought you to a place of intent. Say, "Intention." In other words, whatever is going right or wrong in your life is intentional. Say, "Intentional." God intended for him to leave you. God intended for you to lose that job. God intended for it to hurt you. God intended for you not to understand how it is going to work out. When you are in a place of purpose, you are in a place of God's intent. When God puts you in a place of His intentions, then you will know you are working on a plan with purpose. Where my folk at -- where my folk? I came to tell my folk not to worry about things looking like it is going to destroy you because you are in a place of purpose. As long as you are in a place of purpose, you cannot die. Lean on your neighbor and say, "Neighbor, I can't die! I got to make myself happy. Say, yes Lord!" Say yes, Lord, because whenever He brings you to a place of purpose you have to make yourself happy. I have some sisters and brothers who could stand right now and start

113

to cry, but because you realize that everything is working together, you have to make yourself happy. You must find a way to be happy. Say yes! I need some happy folk. No, wait a minute! I need some folk who don't have anything to be happy about to start praising God right here! I dare you to make yourself happy.

Gideon had to make himself happy with the plan. He didn't like the plan. The plan didn't feel good to him. The plan didn't make sense to him, but he had to find a way to make himself happy. God then complicates the test of Gideon's spirituality. He says, "Gideon?" Gideon says, "Sir?" God tells him, "Don't worry about bows and arrows. Don't worry about swords or shields. You are going to battle with a jar, a trumpet and a candle." Now I am going tell you the truth. I tried to get my hands on about 2000 candles because I was going to give you a candle. But I could not find 2000 of them and I knew if I gave some a candle and didn't give everybody a candle, I'd get beat up. But the next time I preach this, I'm going to give you a candle. Gideon goes to battle with a jar, a trumpet, and a candle. He has divided the men. God has told him that he didn't need any fighting weapons. Can you imagine how Gideon felt? He has to explain to these men that they are going to fight without weapons. Where my folk at? The weapons of our warfare are not carnal, but they are mighty through God to the pulling down of strongholds!

Gideon goes into battle with a musical instrument, a lighted instrument, and a holding instrument. Once you understand that God has a plan, there is nothing the enemy can do to destroy or whip you. God had a plan for Gideon's life. Listen to God as He gives Gideon instructions. He says in verse nine, "I have already delivered the Midianites into your hands." I came for my folk who are thinking that their deliverance is not coming. Before you do battle and walk into the enemy's camp, you must know that God has already given you the victory. So when you go down in the valley to fight the Midianites, you are fighting a battle that you have already won. Where my folk at? You need to know that He has already delivered you. If He said He will save them, and they are smoking crack and drinking liquor, then they are saved!

When God gets through working with you, you will be able to believe God for anything. When I said that God was testing Gideon's faith, I did not mean his faith of things; God was bringing Gideon to the next level of faith. I can believe God just because He is God. I can believe Him while I'm in the middle of some stuff. I am not out of the stuff yet, but I can trust Him while I'm in it. I got anybody in the Nation who is moving to anything? Let me hear you praise Him for "anything" kind of faith. When God started bringing Gideon to an "anything" kind of faith, He says to Gideon, "Get your men and go down to the enemy's camp." Can you imagine Gideon with just 300 fighting men walking down to the enemy's camp? The Lord had sent him to fight an enemy he could not even number, but if you are working with the plan and God is on your side, no weapon formed against you will prosper. Gideon gets those 300 men with a jar, a light, and a trumpet, and they go down to the enemy camp.

According to history, when they start the migration to the enemy camp, it is just breaking evening day, which means the sun was just starting to go down.

But God has something that He calls timing. Look at your neighbor and say, "Neighbor, if you work with the plan, God has a time." God has a time to fix it. He has a time to pull it together. He has a time to bring you out. He has a time to loose your finances. He has a time to heal your body. He has a time to relieve your burden. He has a time. He has a time. Say yes!

The Bible says they went down to the camp when the sun was going down, but God tells Gideon not to do anything yet at somebody and say, "Middle watch." The middle watch would be around 10 p.m. During the middle watch, the Midianites would change the guard. They would move to other positions. The sleeping men would get up and the tired men would go to bed. God said, "Gideon, during the middle watch this is what I want you to do. I want you to blow on your trumpet and when you blow your trumpet tell the other 200 and 99 to blow their trumpets too. While you're blowing your trumpet, hold it in your right hand and take your jar and crack it with the person who is next to you." So Gideon cracked his jar with the soldier that was next to him, and the soldier that was next to him cracked his jar with the soldier that was next to him, and then the soldier that was next to him cracked his jar with the soldier who was next to him. All the Midianites heard was this continuing clashing noise. They heard the sound of the trumpets and they heard the breaking of some glass. Then God said to Gideon, "Hold your light and go to shaking." So the Midianites heard the sound of trumpets, they heard the clanging of breaking glass, and they saw a light that was moving.

The Bible says that when the Midianites started to change the guard all they heard was a thunderous noise.

They saw a shaking light and they got scared. They got scared because out of the midst of the noise Gideon started hollering "The sword of the Lord and the sword of Gideon is coming against you!" Where my folk at? I need for you to throw up your hands and let the devil hear you say it. "The sword of the Lord and the sword of 'insert your own name' is coming against the enemy of the Lord!" The more Gideon hollered, the more the glasses broke and the more the trumpet sounded. The Midianites got so confused they started killing each other. When God gets ready to deliver you, all you have to do is turn it into joy. Turn it into joy! Turn it into joy! Now, ask me how they turned it into joy? When the Israelites were blowing the trumpets and clanging the glass and shaking, they looked down and saw the Midianites killing each other and they began praising God. They went to shaking and they turned it into joy. I came to tell somebody that all you have to do is blow it, break it, shake it, and turn it into joy! Where my folk?!

All Gideon had was the word of deliverance. He rejoiced while deliverance was taking place. I don't want anybody dancing who has already been delivered. I want some blowing, clanging, clashing, screaming, hollering folk to dance because you believe you are GOING to be delivered. You might get home and find folks still acting like a fool, but God said He has already given you deliverance. Come on and blow the trumpets and clash those symbols. I dare you to shake it and turn it into joy!

I'm getting ready to let you go, but let me give you one more thing. You see the devil is just like the Midianites. He thinks he has you right where he can break

117

you, but what the enemy doesn't realize is greater is He that is living in you, and if God said I'm delivered and if God said I'm coming out, then I'm coming out! If God says it is over and if God says it is finished, then I'm going to do just like Gideon. I'm going to start shaking, I'm going to start blowing. I'm going to count those things done. I'm going to dance just like the enemy is already defeated because he is!

Wait a minute, I hear the Holy Ghost saying that you must understand that Gideon didn't have a sword. Gideon didn't have a bow. Gideon didn't have a shield. All Gideon had was enough faith to believe God. My time is coming. I may have a thousand and one folk working against me, but my time is coming, so all I have to do is praise Him. Grab a neighbor by the hand say, "Neighbor, I don't have to live in it, I just got to turn it!"

Work with the plan. Work with what God has intended. Gideon had no idea that the Midianites would be delivered into his hand without a fight. I'm finished, but here is the end of the story. The Midianites had killed so many of each other --it's in the text – that when Gideon went down in the valley there was hardly any enemy left. What looked impossible for 300 men to do was not impossible for God. The Bible says that when the enemy saw the few of them that were left, they started to run in all directions.

Thank you Lord. Thank you for your plan. Thank you for the test of life. When we thought we couldn't, You said we could. When we said no more, You said just a little more. Thank you for the test of life. Thank you for the Word that makes us spiritual. Thank you for the Word that causes us to believe what we cannot see. Thank you for the Word which teaches us to walk after the things of God, knowing that if we say what You say, we will be what You want us to be. Thank you for the plan to test our spirituality. Thank you for the plan that will test our faith. We must move to another level of trusting and believing You. When we come out of this, we will be able to believe You for anything. When we get through with this we will be able to trust You for everything. Thank you for a faith test that will cause us to believe and to see what You have already spoken. Thank you for the ability to blow, to break, and to shake. While the enemy thinks he has got us in his clutches, thank you for enough strength to turn it into joy. We will wait and watch until the full manifestation of that which You have spoken becomes our reality. Our prayer today is one of thanksgiving, one of praise, and one of worship for the plan that You have already designed.

I'm holding on to a sister or a brother. I don't know if they are in the left group, the right group, or if they are working it in the middle. Whatever their position, it is not important. Whatever they are dealing with, that is not important. What is important is that the hand that I touch can turn this situation into joy. So I'm agreeing with this hand today that all things are working together. I'm agreeing with this hand today that what the enemy has meant for evil, God has intent and a purpose to make it good. Bless the hand I touch now. In Jesus name.

A New Lifting

This I recall to my mind therefore I have hope:
[22] Because of the LORD's great love we are not consumed, for his compassions never fail.
[23] They are new every morning; great is your faithfulness.
[24] I say to myself, "The LORD is my portion; therefore I will wait for him."
[25] The LORD is good to those whose hope is in him, to the one who seeks him;
[26] It is good to wait quietly for the salvation of the LORD.
[27] It is good for a man to bear the yoke while he is young.
[28] Let him sit alone in silence, for the LORD has laid it on him.
[29] Let him bury his face in the dust- there may yet be hope.
[30] Let him offer his cheek to one who would strike him, and let him be filled with disgrace.
[31] For men are not cast off by the Lord forever.
[32] Though he brings grief, he will show compassion, so great is his unfailing love.

Lamentations 3:21-32

Today, I am going to talk about *A New Lifting*. Now I'm going to need some prayer warriors for this one because whenever I start talking about sin and repenting, I have to work a little harder to break through to you. But I want you to know I prayed and I'm ready for you. Today, I came with you in mind.

By way of introduction, not only for today's message but perhaps an introduction to the Book of Lamentations for most of you, we must take a look back in order to understand Jeremiah's plight as he writes this book of poems in Lamentations. We must look back in order to understand why Jeremiah is lamenting in the first place. The Book of Lamentations is Jeremiah's book of warning. He is, in fact, crying and weeping. In looking back at Jeremiah and his dilemma, we discover that Jeremiah is crying over the destruction of Jerusalem.

A brief historical account confirms that Jeremiah is upset because Jerusalem has been destroyed. The capitol city of Judah, the southern kingdom, has been utterly damaged by Nebuchadnezzar and the Babylonian army. It has been destroyed to the point that the walls have been torn down and the city is exposed with no arena of protection. Not only did Nebuchadnezzar and his armies tear down the walls, but they also torched the temple and burned down and desecrated their place of worship. The destruction of the city was so devastating that all Jeremiah could do was cry. Can you imagine it? Just take a moment to remember all that went down on 9/11, with the towers burning and tumbling and crashing down. Can you imagine a whole city crumbling before your eyes? Can you imagine an entire city going down in rumble? That was Jeremiah's dilemma. The city was crumbling before his very eyes and all Jeremiah could do was weep and cry.

Jeremiah had been warned by God that judgment was inevitable and that judgment was coming to the people of God. Actually seeing it, however, was more than Jeremiah could bear. God had warned the people through Jeremiah that their offerings and their sacrifices were now stinking in His nostrils, and nothing they could do or say would shift God's hand of judgment. The people had an opportunity to turn from their wicked ways and stop breaking God's laws, but because they insisted on sinning, God was fed up. He was sending a judgment.

Let's pause there a moment. America is vastly moving toward the very same sad epithet. God has sent warning after warning that if America as a nation does not cut out some of its foolishness and its sinning, we will suffer for it. God is going to send a judgment on America. Well, you know me; I ain't scared of anybody up in here. We do not hear it preached. We hear about prosperity and the promises of God and all of that is true, but prosperity and the promises of God will never take the place of God's judgment. If you think that God is not going to judge us because of sin, you are crazy. Jeremiah watched God's judgment fall upon Jerusalem. In the midst of God's judgment falling upon Jerusalem, all Jeremiah could do was weep and cry. Out of Jeremiah's tears and frustration, he journals what we call the Book of Lamentations. It is a book of poems that Jeremiah wrote to ease his frustration and his fear.

For those of you who do not journal, journaling is a wonderful way to record your prophecy and your state of being. Journaling can be a source of comfort and hope. It can inspire you. Write it down! Make it plain! Keep it before you. Journaling has a way of releasing deeply felt emotions. Your journal is your personal story. It is your testament of what is going on, what has gone on, and what you feel about what is happening to you.

In the Book of Lamentations, Jeremiah expresses his heartache at seeing the city burning and totally destroyed and the heartache which followed that devastation. He also expressed his experience of faith as he penned his journal of Lamentations. Let's park there for a moment. You have to have your own experience of faith. I cannot live your faith. I cannot develop your faith. If you are going to believe and trust God, you will have to make up your mind to do just that. Journaling allows you to write about your own experience of faith. It is hard to trust God if God has never done anything for you. However, when you revisit your journal and you read about the things that God has done for you, you can gain hope, comfort and expectation.

It is amazing to me that while in the midst of difficult situations and terribly painful times, I have experienced some of the most profound levels of faith. Anybody agree with me? I have experienced tremendous faith while facing tremendous obstacles. It is strange how faith kicks in when you are at your lowest point. After the judge has given the sentence and the doctor has given the diagnosis, I have had tremendous experiences with faith. In our text, Jeremiah is developing profound faith at the same time he is experiencing intense heartache and pain. Through the heartache and pain, Jeremiah realizes God. During the most difficult of times, Jeremiah's faith is stretched beyond what he feels he can bear.

In the third chapter of Lamentations, we pick up Jeremiah's life as an old man. By the time he journals chapter three in Lamentations, he has experienced all kinds of suffering and he has felt all kinds of pain. Yet here in our text, he has come to some realities about how God operates and God's processes. You do know that God has a process and God's process has a purpose. God doesn't just do stuff to be doing it. Any time God allows something to happen, God has a specific reason for it happening. When God deals with a people or with a person, you can tell if you've grieved God. You do know that you can cause God grief? As much as God loves human beings, human beings can get on God's last nerve.

At the time of our text, Jeremiah has come to understand something about human nature and how we relate to God. Jeremiah says that when you find yourself in trouble with God and you are at the blunt end of God's judgment, there are few things you need to do. The first thing Jeremiah says you need to do is remember. Look at your neighbor and say, "Remember." Jeremiah says when you find yourself in trouble with God, you need to think about what got you in trouble with God in the first place. You need to realize that something, someone, some situation, or some activity that you were involved in, got you in the mess in the first place. You need to remember. I knew I was going to have to work, so I came to work. I arose early this morning and prayed. There is somebody in Calvary today that needs to remember why you are in the mess you are in right now. This is your day to remember.

Now to remember means that you have to bring it up in your mind again. Some of us have been involved in so much stuff that we are part of the cover up gang. You come here to shout, dance, holler and scream, but all you are doing is covering it up. Well, I'm going to bust it wide open tonight. I'm going to go to work on that demon right here and now. I will make you remember! If God is not blessing you maybe it is because of something you are into. Lord, help me right here. Help me, Jesus. You need to recall. You need to reminisce. You need to recollect. You need to think about it again. You need to revisit your own situation and remind yourself why you are still dealing with the same stuff. You need to check yourself. Don't worry about who is not here. God has YOU here. This one is for you. Don't worry about the folks who are on your row or the folks you think should hear this message. You are here! This one is for you.

You need to check yourself and find out why the blessings of God are not upon your life. Maybe it is because of something or someone you are involved with and that is the reason why you are missing God. Lord, help me. Let me serve notice on you. When you really check yourself, you will find something. You cannot check yourself and come up with an A+ on everything. There's no way, sugar. When you check yourself, you will find that there are some shortcomings in you! When we talk about a *"New Lifting"* that indicates there was something to be lifted from. Something has caused you to be misplaced with God. Oh, it is a bit tight, but you ain't going to sleep on me! You might as well just wake up!

Jeremiah says you need to repent and he is weeping. He is weeping because Jerusalem should have known better. Lord, help me. God had made His laws plain. God said, *"Thou shall not."* It wasn't that Jerusalem was ignorant of the laws. They just decided to do their own thing in spite of the law. Lord, help me. If you think that you can call yourself Christian and do your own thing and God not send a judgment on your life, you are a maniac! God is not playing with you! If He said the soul that sins shall die, then honey, the soul that sins shall die! I know you don't like it. If God said the wages of sin is death, honey, the wages of sin is death!

We have allowed folks to be weak. Lord, help me! You cannot afford to have a weakness in your life. A weakness is an arrow that will send you straight to the bull's eye of sin. A weakness is nothing but you compromising with yourself. I say if I must live holy, you have to live holy too. If it is good for the goose then it's good for the gander. Oh, you don't want to hear this, but I came to talk to you. I have a few folk who are praying for me. God is not putting up with sin in the pulpit, and he will not put up with sin in the pew! I said He is not going to put up with it! No sin in the pulpit and none in the pew either. I ain't scared of you. You'll never say you didn't hear it. I'm telling you, you need to remember. If God delivered you out of anything, God can deliver you out of everything. I'm working on a demon up in here today.

Sin is a reproach against God. He loves sinners but He hates sin, and He does not expect you to continue in sin. Paul said, "What shall we say to these things oh retched man that I am? Shall I continue in sin that grace may abound?" You try to trap God by saying that you are going to sin because His grace is there and He is faithful and just and that if we confess our sins, He will forgive us. Are you trying to make the Word of God of no effect and continue in sin? God is going to send a judgment in your life! Here is your warning. Cut it out! I said cut it out! God will not send an angel down here and close up all the liquor stores so you won't drink. He will not stop making good-looking women -- me included -- so you can keep your zipper up. You need some self-control!

You need to remember the same God who extends mercy and love is also fair and just. You cannot talk about His love and His mercy without talking about His fairness and His justice. If you are in sin, you are breaking the laws of God and you will be judged. Thank you, Jesus. I don't care if "everybody's doing something" because that is a lie from the pit of hell. You mean we have an El Shadai all mighty God and He does not have one person on earth that can live free from sin? That devil is a lie. You are a lie. You just like telling that lie so you can keep on doing what you are doing, but there are holy people. Everybody does not have their hand in the cookie jar. Some of us have made up our mind not to touch it, not to taste it, and not to handle anything that is unclean. I can't get anybody to praise Him right here. Where are the holy folks? Do I have any holy folks in here?

You know why we have a praise team and why they sing for 30 minutes? Because some of you have to repent every time you go to God. So the praise teams have to sing for 30 minutes, then the minister has to get up here and exalt for another 15 minutes, so you can finally emerge into a right place with God. Wonder what service would be like if just 75% of us came in here and didn't have to repent?

That is my second point. After you remember, you need to repent. Oh, see you can't even say it. You need to repent! That is what Jeremiah is saying. You need to repent. Now let me tell you something about repentance. Repentance is not coming up to this altar crying. That's a sorry somebody . . . you just sorry . . . and the harder you cry, the sorrier you are, but that is no indication that you have repented. Let me tell you about real repentance. Real repentance will cause you to change your life style. So about 80% of you have never really repented because real repentance says this to God, "I don't want to touch it, I don't want to be with him, I don't want anything to do with it, and if I look like I'm going to do it again, take me out of here!" Look at the few folk standing up. Why? Because some of you want to negotiate. Oh, I came for you today. I came for you.

Yes, some of you want to negotiate. Well, that is not real repentance because real repentance says I will not touch it ever again in life. If I have to go to bed with a teddy bear or if I have get on my house phone and call my cell phone, I will not talk to you no more! Help me Jesus! Help me up in here! Help me in here! I'm talking about repentance! Look at your neighbor and tell your neighbor, "You need to repent." You need to make a decision to quit it! You need to make a decision to be through with it and stop seesawing back and forth. If you are under it, get over it! You weren't born with it and you can live without it. You are not the only single person in the world and you are not the only single momma. Half of the people in here are single parents. You are not the only one that somebody did something wrong to. Get over it! Stop harboring that weakness and get over it. Repent! Holler back, "Repent!"

We have people in the church who have been in church for ten years still holding on to something. Are you crazy? Do you think it takes God ten years to get you out of something? I said do you think it takes God ten years to get you out of sin? My father was a habitual smoker for 45 years. Two weeks after he gave his life to the Lord, he stopped drinking, smoking and chasing women. You just need to repent. I came for you today. You are in it because you want to be. You hang with them because you want to. As soon as you cut them loose, they will cut you loose and talk about you while they're cutting you loose. I'd rather you talk about me and let me get over you than to receive the judgment of God. Talk about me, honey. Talk!

When one really repents you change your attitude and with that change of attitude is a change of mindset. With that change of mindset there are changes in your life style. That is why nobody believes you are saved. You talk Christian, but you don't walk Christian. There is a big difference in talking Christian and walking Christian. That's why folk are confused about you because you say one thing, but your lifestyle does not measure up with your big mouth talk. So we don't know who you are. Wait, but wait a minute, yes we do. You know how you can tell you got rodents? You can smell them. They start stinking and then there are all those droppings. You talk Christian but you're not walking Christian. You need to change your lifestyle. And you need to do it today before God sends a judgment.

That is a real prophecy! You don't even know real prophesy when you hear it. I am not talking about a car. I am not talking about a Mercedes or a five bedroom house. I am talking about sin. Here is a prophecy. I am prophesying good right now. I am not talking about you becoming a millionaire. Here is real prophecy! Sin is a reproach against God. Give me a hand for prophecy. Here is another prophecy. You better straighten yourself up and you better come out of sin before God sends a judgment in your life and tears down everything that you are trying to build up. You better repent! Give me a hand for prophecy. If you still doing the same ol' same ol' that you been doing since you got saved; if you walk out of these doors and still smoking and still drinking; or if you walk out of here and still sleep with him or her or a combination of both, you better repent. Didn't I tell you I ain't scared of you? I ain't scared of you! If you walk out of here and still say it, if you leave here and go straight to it, or if you walk out and still play it, you have not repented from it. I am working it today, but that's okay. You'll never dance and jump up in here and say you never heard about repentance.

Jeremiah said you need to remember, and after you remember what got you here in the first place, you need to repent. And do not cover up your weakness. The Bible says come out from among them, and be ye separate. You cannot live a life that pleases God until you separate yourself from sin. And let me serve notice on all of you who are trying to separate but still hang around sinners. Now, I'm not saying that all your running buddies are in sin. Oh yeah, I guess I am saying that. I'm not saying that you can't go to the Safeway unless the cashier is saved or that you can't go to Wal-Mart (y'all know I love Wal-Mart) unless everybody in there is speaking in tongues. I am not suggesting that at all. What I am suggesting is that your close associates, those people that you are in relationship and fellowship with, need to be Christians.

I do not understand how you can have fellowship with somebody who is not loving God. I just don't understand it! And help me to understand why the weak bunch hang around weak folk? When weak folk get with other weak folk, they don't ever want to pray. They don't ever have anything good to say about anybody and they are always talking against the program, downing the president, and talking against the ministry. How can you have so much in common with somebody like that?

Jeremiah says you need to remember and if you are going to move to this next level and not receive God's judgment, you need to repent. Maybe the thing that is holding up your blessing and breakthrough is you. Maybe it is not the devil. Maybe the thing or the person that is stopping God's hand of blessing on your life is you. The Bible is true through and through. Be not deceived, God is not mocked. Whatever you sow, you will reap. We don't sing it anymore but I loved it when we were singing it. I gave it up, that's when He blessed me. Turned it loose, that's when He blessed me. I let it go, that's when He blessed me. You need to think about what you are holding on to. You need to think about who you do not want to let go of. You need to think about what you do not want to turn loose. Because maybe the very moment that you make up your mind to walk away from it, that is when God will open up the windows of heaven and pour you out a blessing. Slap your neighbor a five and say, "Turn it loose!" Slap that neighbor on the other side a five and say, "Let it go!" Turn around and slap that neighbor behind you and tell them, "Give it up so God can bless you!" Say yes!

Verse 21 picks up as Jeremiah says, "I recalled it." In other words, I remembered what God said to Judah. I recalled the laws that God had set up and when I recalled it, when it came to my mind again, I remembered what God had said. I realized that the destruction and devastation we were dealing with was of our own doing. Verse 21 continues with ". . . but then there was hope."

Jeremiah says I remembered it, I recalled it, but as I was remembering and recalling, I discovered there was hope for me and hope for us. He says I repented when I remembered it and verse 22 says, "*I realized it is of the Lords mercies that I was not consumed because his compassions fail not.*"

We hear that quote all the time, but that quote was said when Jeremiah realized that Judah had sinned. They had almost come to a place of repentance, but God was so merciful and had so much compassion that while they were sinning, He didn't kill them. I'm going to help somebody up in here! It is going to take a real honest group of folks to stand up and give God some praise because you know that while you were doing it, He did not take you out of here. You better praise Him because He let you live. He kept you alive when you did not deserve it. It was because of the Lord's mercies that you were not consumed. It is not that you did not do it. It is because of His mercy. He did not allow it to consume you because His compassion failed not and is new every morning.

Some of you need to get real happy because you did it last year and He still let you walk into 2002. Some of you did it last night, but thank God, there are new mercies every morning! You need to praise Him for new mercy. Help me Jesus! I repeat . . . you need to get glad for new mercy. You need to be glad that it was not old mercy, but He woke you up to a brand new mercy.

Jeremiah said, "I remembered and I repented." I discovered that he should have let this happen a long time ago, but because He had mercy and because God is full of compassion, when I should have been written off, when it should have caught up with me, and when I should have been exposed, He covered me with compassion. I know you are in here! You don't want to signify and get happy, but I know you are here. Do I have about 50 more folks who know you are alive because God covered you? You have smoked it since you were saved. You snorted it since you were saved, but He covered you!

Jeremiah said it was because of the Lord's mercies and His compassion that he was alive. The only reason why we have not been consumed is because He is faithful to us. Lord, have mercy. hen I wasn't walking faithful to Him, He was faithful toward me. Don't you get up here looking sanctimonious like you have been with Jesus every day since you were saved? At least be truthful today. You know God covered you! You know He has been better to you than you have been to yourself. You know He has been faithful even when you were not walking faithfully with Him. Clap your hands and praise Him for His faithfulness. His mercies are new every morning. Great is God's faithfulness.

Jeremiah continues, "The Lord is my portion. He will not cast me off forever." Because I have repented, the Lord will have compassion on me. I made up my mind I am going to get through one way or the other. I made up my mind some years ago that I am going to live for God. If there is anything in the Bible that says you can be holy, I will be holy. I made up my mind. If this thing doesn't work, it will not be because I did not live it. I made up my mind that God has no respect of person. Any and every body who names the name of the Lord can walk up right and talk to God. If Paul had a relationship with Him, I'm going to have one. If Peter had a relationship with Him, I'm going to have one. If Mary was called blessed among

134

women, then I'm going to be called blessed. I need somebody who really means to walk with God to praise Him right here. Open up your mouth and praise the living God!

The last thing Jeremiah says is "He will have compassion on me according to the multitudes of his mercies." He says, "Once I realized, I remembered and repented." Make a change in the direction of my life. Then you will be able to make a proper response. You cannot remember and you cannot really repent without making some kind of a response. To respond means to make a return by some action. To respond means to react favorably. So here in verse 40 and 41 is Jeremiah's response. He says, "I searched and I repented . . . and acknowledged my way and turned again to the Lord." Verse 41 has his response. He says, "Let us lift up our hearts with our hands unto God." In other words Jeremiah says, let us respond and invoke God's presence in a new dimension in our lives. Let's give God an opportunity for a new lifting in our spirits. He says let's invoke God so we can feel a new thing in us . . . a fresh portion of God's spirit . . . a fresh presence of the Lord's spirit . . . a fresh anointing . . . a higher portion . . . a deeper position. Lord, lift me up where I belong. Lift me above the temptation. Lift me beyond the tribulation. Lift me out of the trouble so I can serve you with gladness of heart. Take me out of the hurt. Lift me above the pain. Let my life please you in such a way that I'll constantly feel your presence. Lift me to a new place.

I don't know where you are in this building, but I know God is beginning a work on somebody's heart, mind, and spirit to give you a new lift. You realize you cannot serve God with sin in your life. In just a moment I am going to give you an opportunity to repent because you remember. The mess you are in is of your own doing, but thanks be to God for He will give us the victory when we make up our mind that we are going to turn away from sin.

God will show up when you set it up. You want to know that God is real? You want to know that God can do what God says He can do? I dare you to set it up. If you set it up and if you come clean with God, He will know when you really mean it. When you set it up, I promise you He is going to show up. God will show up and give you enough strength to stay clean from that thing that you walk away from, or the person or the place that you walk away from. A *New Lifting* . . . God is going to give you a new lifting.

Prepare to Go the Distance

⁵And as he lay and slept under a juniper tree, behold, then an angel touched him, and said unto him, Arise and eat.
⁶And he looked, and, behold, there was a cake baken on the coals, and a cruse of water at his head. And he did eat and drink, and laid him down again.
⁷And the angel of the LORD came again the second time, and touched him, and said, Arise and eat; because the journey is too great for thee.

I Kings 19:5-7

Come on and put your hands together if you love the Lord. Come on and clap those hands like you love Jesus. Amen. Before you take your seats glance over at your neighbor and say, "Neighbor, you're sitting beside the right one." Amen. Let's look at the Word of the Lord.

I had a nice little time with this sermon in the 8:45 service, but I did not get to finish. This time, I hope to get to the end. Let us look at I Kings, chapter 19. I would just like to reiterate a couple of the scriptures and then we will move into the Word of the Lord. Glance over at your neighbor and repeat my subject after me say, "Neighbor, oh neighbor, *Prepare to Go the Distance.*" Look at your neighbor on the other side and say, "That's what we are going to talk about." Look back at your neighbor on the other side and say, "Neighbor, did you hear what I said? You need to *Prepare to Go the Distance.*" Now put your hand on yourself. Sometimes you have to signify by talking to yourself. Talk to yourself and say, "Self, this is my day and my time to prepare myself to go the distance." Amen. Clap your hands as you take your seats.

By way of introduction, the Books of First and Second Kings provide us believers spiritual lessons which have timeless value. The Books of First and Second Kings gives us lessons which transcend time in their significance and importance as we seek to do God's will. For example, in the Books of Kings we are shown how God revealed Himself and His message to the people of Israel. We see how God instigated and taught them about who He was. God accomplished this through his servants. They were known as prophets. That's a good place to park for a minute. We have so many people today who claim to be prophets. Well you know I wasn't scared of them this morning, and I ain't scared of you neither! Some people claim to be spokespersons for God. They say it is God who has instructed them to say or to do whatever it is they are saying or doing. My problem with the prophets of today is that they all seem to hear from God concerning houses, land, clothes and jewelry. I just wonder if God has anything else to talk about.

Now I am not against houses and land and all of those kinds of things. Certainly, we are living in a day where we can be more prosperous than we have ever been in our lives. But has God's message to us been reduced to what kind of car you driving, what kind of house you living in, and what designer label is in the back of your dress or suit? I think not. I think God has a little more to say than that. Certainly, today's prophets get a round of applause when they start naming husbands and wives. I am not against relationships; certainly not one that includes marriage. However, if your entire spiritual existence is contingent upon whether you marry or not, you have a problem. I said you have a problem! God has something else to say other than when you will get married and who you are going to get married to. I know it is Valentine's Day, but honey, if you are not happy by yourself, you sure enough can't be happy with someone else. Oh, you all don't want to hear no preaching! I see I am going to have to work. You all pray for me because I'm going to have to work up in here!

We have people who call themselves Christians who are going crazy because they have to go home alone. There is nothing wrong with going home alone. As much as I love the Bishop, sometimes he can get on my last nerve. That boy gets on my last nerve! At home alone sounds good to me sometime. Come on married folks! Home alone is not such a bad idea. I know you're all "lovey-dovey" right now, but there comes a time when you want him or her to go. Sometimes you want to say take you and your stuff up out of here!

I think God's prophets ought to have a little more substance in their messages. I am not saying that God does not speak about those kinds of things, but if everything is "money cometh," if everything is what you drive and where you live, what message does that convey? God is never reduced to materialistic things. The fact that you drive, live, and enjoy the finer things of life is no indication that you have a relationship with God. Drug dealers and embezzlers enjoy the finer things too. Come on! You have to learn to be happy with what God has blessed you with and do not let any body prophesy over you something that you know is not true. You know that joker is prophesying a lie to you, yet you just sit there and say, "Yes, Lord." You know it's a lie! You know you're not healed! You still in pain! Don't tell me you claiming something while you sit there hurting. We have given prophets too much liberty and we have not made them accountable. Don't worry about me. When y'all were sacrificing your jewelry and stuff, I had _all_ my stuff on. I didn't take off one bracelet, one earring, one nothing. Go ahead and play the video. I had all my stuff on and walked out with everything still intact.

There was a difference in how Elijah and prophets during his time prophesized. Their prophecies brought the children of Israel into some accountability with their conduct and their behavior. You think God will give you all these blessings and you shacking and living like the devil? That is not going to happen. You smoking, clubbing, and running around town and you think you can say, "Yes Lord, give it to me." You need to sit down! Elijah brought the children of Israel into some type of accountability. Those who are sent by God must first tell you what God has said according to His Word as it relates to your walk with Him. You will not need a Mercedes or a Bentley in heaven. We will have wings. Amen. You won't need to take any gold to heaven. The record says the streets in heaven are made of pure gold. God must bring you into some accountability with your life style. Your conduct should be in God's favor. In other words, you should be walking, living and talking God's laws and standards.

Elijah, Elisha and the other prophets of that time brought people to a place of accountability as they dealt with their disobedience. God does not bless disobedient people. I knew nobody was going to say Amen to that. So let me say it again. God does not bless disobedient people. He is not going to shower down on you His blessings and you are walking around doing whatever it is you feel you're big enough and bad enough to do. God blesses individuals who believe in Him and who obey His Word. I can't get a clap right there, but that is okay.

The Books of Kings also show us the faithfulness of God as it relates to how God will honor His Word and His promises. I like to put it this way: it shows us how God honors His "Word promises." You see, some people just have promises, but other people have Word promises. In other words, somebody has spoken a direct word to you from the Lord and in that word there are some direct promises. That is a Word promise. It will not, as the Bible states, return unto God void. Whatever God's Word promise is to you, God is going to accomplish that word and the Books of Kings show us the faithfulness of God in completing what God had promised. God had promised their forefathers a land that flowed with milk and honey. God had promised their forefathers that the seed lineage line would be blessed and the Book of Kings describes the kind of Word promises that were to flow to the children of Israel.

To understand the concept of Word promises fully, you have to look at the backdrop of the text which tells us that Ahab was the king. You know that famous girl Jezebel? She was the queen. So the people had to rely on God's Word promises in the middle of all kinds of wicked situations. But Elijah tells us as he told them; God is faithful concerning His promises towards us. God's hand and arm are not short. Whatever He says, God is faithful to complete. All you have to do is obey and walk after the ways of God. You have to know what God has given you and that you are dealing with a purpose. Everybody say, "Purpose." God's purpose will come to pass.

I need for you to understand that in order for you to be blessed, in order for you to reach your blessed time in God; you have to go through some experiences. I know about the cliché that says experience is not the best teacher, but I'm telling you that experience will teach you something. Can I get a witness? Usually before God blesses you, your blessing is preceded by an experience. It is impossible to know God until you have had some kind of an experience with God. I dare say that at least 40% of you sitting in here have not had an encounter or experience with the Lord. Once you have an experience with God, certain knowledge and practical wisdom is gained from what you observed or encountered. Some of you are so busy trying to get out of your situations that God cannot teach you anything. Everything that happens to you or displeases you is not necessarily of the devil. I said everything that happens to you that doesn't make you shout, jump or bump may not be of the devil! It may be an experience whereby God is trying to teach you something. You have to learn to bend and lean not to your own understanding, but in all your ways acknowledge Him so that He can teach you something. Point your finger in your neighbor's face and say, "Neighbor, the Lord is trying to teach you something."

You have to undergo certain things. You have to have certain encounters. You have to skin your knee, bust your nose, put your arm in a sling and put a cast on your leg so that you will know who and what God is and what

He is capable of doing. You don't really know God until you have had an experience with Him and the best experiences are often painful. You don't know He can put bread on your table unless you've had some hunger pains. Somebody better help me up in here! You don't know that He is a doctor in a sick room and a lawyer in a court room unless you've gone to the doctor and he declared there was something growing in your body and he didn't know how to get it out. You don't know that He can make a way out of no way and bless you in the process, unless you experience Him. You got to have an experience! There is no way you can fully comprehend God unless God brings you through something.

If God were to roll back the clouds and put His presence in the sky, you would have cardiac arrest. There is no way you can see God and live. God's glory is too great. God's glory is too brilliant. When Moses was up on the hillside and took just a glance at God's backside, he had to veil his face for 40 days because people couldn't even look on him. God cannot show you who He is! You can't take it. That is why He gives you an experience. You cannot fully believe God until you have experienced Him. You cannot believe in a God who you cannot see unless something in your life connects you to Him?

You have got to have a connection with God. There are people praising God with no connection to Him. People are worshiping God with no connection to Him. People are preaching with no connection to Him. If you want to know God, you got to get connected. I need to hear a praise right there! Help me, Jesus! The old folk used to say, "You can't make me doubt Him. I know too much about Him." Anytime people get to weeping, waving and flickering at the first sign of trouble, I wonder about how connected they are to God. Anybody ought to be able to stand a little bit of trouble, but we got people in the church that don't want <u>any</u> trouble. Do you really think you will sail all the way from earth to glory and not experience any hardship? You a crazy somebody!

Everything that I've ever read in the Bible says we will go through trials and tribulations. I don't care who comes on the television or the radio and tells you that you will not have any trouble or any hard times, and that you are not going to have any struggles, they are liars! Jesus said if you live in this present world you will have tribulations! I can't get anybody to believe it! Trials and tribulations are what gives you experience. You do not learn things when everything is going well. You learn in adversity! You don't know that He will make ends meet if every bill you got is paid on time with money left over. I need somebody in here who doesn't have enough money to do squat, yet you still in your apartment and you still have gas,. . . you better give Him a praise!

The experience is what qualifies you for the blessing. Lord, I just said something good right there. I said the experience is what qualifies you for the blessing. That is why you are not blessed. You haven't had enough experiences to qualify you! God is not just going to open up the windows of heaven, turn on the light, and just pour blessings down on you because you asked for it. You are not the only one asking for it! What makes you different from everybody else on the row is what you have been through. I don't care if I never preach at another coliseum, I'm qualified. I have been through enough to tell anybody

"The Lord will make a way some how!" Slap that neighbor a five and say, "I'm qualified for this blessing! You better move out my way because I'm going to get it – I'm qualified!"

Elijah was qualified. Elijah knew that he was God's man. You have to know that you are God's man or woman. It does not matter what anybody else thinks. You see, some of you cannot get a really good blessing because you have got too many people with you. You've got prayer partners, the whole usher board, and all the ministers praying for you. You've got mentors from North Carolina to New Jersey! So when God gets ready to bless you, He has to divide the blessing up. He has to give some of the blessing to her because she was the one who prayed you through on Tuesday. He has to give some of the blessing to another one because she was the one who prayed you through on Thursday. He has to give some of it to him over there because he laid hands on you when you came to the altar on Sunday. He has to give some of it to her over yonder and that whole little group because they were the ones who said you would be blessed. That is why you do not have a good blessing. I want to be like Elijah. I will struggle through and beat the devil. If I have to step on his head, cry all night, and fast all day in order to get my blessing, I'll do it! That devil is a liar!

I like Elijah. He was up on the hillside by himself. If you want to have a real experience with God, you must get in a place alone with Him! Slap your neighbor a high five and say, "Go for yourself by yourself." Look at the neighbor on the other side and tell them the same thing, say "Go for yourself by yourself!" You have to look in the mirror and tell yourself, "I can handle this." I am the man or the woman for the job. God knows all there is to know about me and I can walk in this. I can hold on. I may have to hold on with sweaty hands. I may have to hold on with blackened eyes, but I can handle this! I did not come this far to fail! But listen, when you do not have any experiences and you have not struggled through anything, you are like a spoiled child. Every time you wanted a pair of tennis shoes, you got them, whether they were Jordan's or whoever else's name was supposed to be on them. Whenever you needed something, somebody got it for you. You do not know anything about struggle! You do not know anything about surviving! But when you struggle for everything you have and when you work hard night and day, you can appreciate what you get!

I am a survivor because I struggled through, and there isn't a devil in hell that can make me take it back. I need some survivors to jump up and holler, "I am a survivor!" Say yes! Hallelujah! I made it! I have the bruises to prove it. You do not know how it feels to be talked about unless you've been talked about in a struggle. You do not know how it feels to be laughed at unless you've been laughed at during a struggle. You do not know what it is like to sing the blues in the night when it is midnight all day long. If you made it through, you got a right to be blessed! Say yes! Lord, have mercy.

Elijah was up on the mountain alone. Picture the setting. There were 450 prophets on the other side and another 400 preachers, which made it 850 against one, but when you have had one good experience with the Lord! It is just like having a good cry. Some of you haven't had a real good cry. There is a difference in a cry and a really good cry. Now a cry will go something like this, "weep, sniff, and a little dab." But a good cry goes something like this, "choke, scream, a big convulsion and OH GOD!" When you have one of those good cries, there is nobody there to pat you on the back. You are there all by yourself. Lord, help me. When you are hurting, you don't want to hear anybody saying "calm down, shut up, or you talking too loud." No! **You** shut up! Don't tell me not to holler! I'm going to look right at you and scream my head off. Anybody in here know what I'm talking about?

The Bible says Elijah was up on the mountain alone. The rules of the contest were very simple. The God who answered by fire would be declared God. No problem. Elijah allowed the opposing team to go first. After all, there was so many of them. So they started at sunrise and, according to ancient customs from sunrise to almost sunset, they called on the name of their gods. They called on Cembalo, the male God, and on Astron, the feminine god, but no fire lit the altar. What I love about God is He will give the enemy enough time to make a fool of himself. Some of you are fussing at God, but you need to be happy because He is giving the devil just enough time to make a fool out of himself. Elijah then says, "Around this evening sacrifice it will be my turn." There wouldn't be any discussion about how, and when, and why the fire came. Elijah instructed that trenches be dug around the altar and that the altar wood be wet. He was confident the fire would come.

You have to be confident not only in God, but you have to be confident in the God in you. Some of you believe in the God in me, but you don't believe in the God in you! The problem with that is it won't work for you because it can only work according to the faith that worketh in you. If you don't have any faith working in you, God cannot do what He wants to do in you. Why? Because you don't believe He can do it.

The Bible says Elijah told them to fill up the trenches and wet the altar and then he turned his face toward the eastern sun and said, "The God of Abraham, the God of Isaac, and the God of Jacob, hear me today. Show yourself by fire." Now if you've ever had God show up in any form, then you have got to believe He can show up in <u>every</u> form. If He showed up in a cloud, He can show up in fire. If He showed up in water, He can show up in fire. If He showed up in wine, He can show up in whatever form He chooses. It does not matter what form because it is the power behind the form. The Bible says that immediately as Elijah finished praying, fire fell from heaven and consumed the altar. Elijah had an experience with God which qualified him for a blessing.

There are three things I want to tell you and then I'm finished. Elijah had to learn three things in order to prepare himself to go the distance. He struggled through the process of experience. Tell yourself, "I'm struggling through the process of an experience." He struggled always to obey. Say to yourself, "I'm struggling through the process of obedience." Then he sits down under a juniper tree or a broom tree. A broom tree was about 12 feet high and known for its large leaves which gave shade and shadow. Elijah sits down under the broom tree and it should have shaded him, but how many of you know that when God gets ready to bring you to a place of blessing, He will find you and bring you to the place where He

148

wants you to be. You cannot hide from God!

The Bible says Elijah sits down under the tree and before God talks to him, God messes with him first. Look at your neighbor and say, "God is going to mess with you right now." God messes with Elijah by allowing him to engage in some unnecessary jargon. Listen to Elijah's jargon. "Lord, you might as well take me. I'm the only one of your prophets left. I'm sitting under this tree and I really don't feel like dealing with what I've got to deal with, so why don't you just change this situation and let me out."

I have come to tell you today that God is not going to let you out of anything that He wants you to experience. You must learn how to stay with it. Lean on your neighbor and say, "Neighbor, stay in it." I know it doesn't feel good, but stay in it. I know it doesn't taste good, but stay in it. God is bringing you to a place of blessing and you've got to prepare yourself to go the distance. God is trying to teach you something so that when He blesses you, you will have learned your lesson. Don't you allow the enemy to destroy or discredit what God is trying to do in you because you so busy fussing in it. You have to learn to throw up your hands and hold up your head and say, "Have thine own way, Lord." Thou art the potter and we are the clay. You must learn to look in the mirror and tell yourself, "If God thought I couldn't handle it, then God would not have allowed it. God must see something in me that I cannot see in myself." It is a mighty fine feeling to know that God sees something in you that you cannot see in yourself.

The next level of blessing is going to require

something from you. Grab your neighbor and shake that hand real good and say, "Neighbor, this next level of blessing will require something from you." Anybody can get just any old kind of blessing, but if you are trying to get the very, very best that God has for you, you are going to have to walk with God through the fire and flood. You will have to walk with God through the storm and the rain. I declare unto you that if you stay in it, the Lord has a way to make what was meant for evil turn around and bless you. The Lord has a way! So what the enemy meant to destroy you, God will use to bring you out. I hear the Holy Ghost saying, "Eyes have not seen and ears have not heard." You cannot imagine what God has in store for you.

You have to learn how to do it like Jesus did. If God tells you to walk to the left and take three spins, honey, I don't care who is laughing and I don't care who pokes fun at you, you better walk to the left and take three spins. If God tells you to hit it in the middle, I don't care who says you can't and I don't care who believes you can't, you take yourself and hit it straight in the middle. If God says go to the right and walk around it seven times, everybody in the building can look at you like you are crazy, but you better go to the right and walk around it seven times. Just as sure as God said it, He is setting you up for a blessing and you have to be prepared to go the distance. Lean on your neighbor's shoulder and say, "Neighbor, I'm getting ready to do it like the Lord says. I'm preparing myself for a blessing. I don't know when and I don't know how. I don't know where and I don't know who. However, what I do know is my faith looks up to thee."

The Bible says that Jezebel and Ahab got angry because when God answered by fire, 850 prophets were killed, and Jezebel got an attitude. She sends a message to Elijah saying, "I swear by this time tomorrow in 24 hours you will be dead. I swear to you and I make you a vow that in 24 hours your prophets will be mine." How dare the devil give God an ultimatum!

Somebody in Calvary today has been given an ultimatum by the devil. He told you, "If you don't do what I say, I'm going to set you outdoors. If you don't do what I say, I'm going to stop giving you money." How dare the enemy of my soul give my God an ultimatum! Slap three people a five and say, "You don't know who you are messing with!" You don't know what I've come through. You don't know how hurt I've been. I've already been frustrated. I've already been disappointed. I've already been discouraged. I've already been lied on. I've already been talked about. There is nothing you can say about me that has not been said already. I've already been called a whore. I've already been called a bitch. Everything has been said that can be said and there is nothing you can say to make me feel bad. I have a God who says if I trust Him all things are passed away. Say yes!

I need to hear praise in this house. Open up your mouth and clap your hands. I need to hear you praise Him. I need to hear you praise Him. I need to hear some praise. I'm a candidate for a blessing. I paid my dues. I said I paid my dues! Don't make me angry with you . . . I paid for it. I paid for every car I will ride in. I paid for every mink coat I will put on my body. I paid for every diamond ring. Don't be jealous of me. I already paid for it! I have

151

been exhausted and frustrated. I've already had too many prayers not answered. I already looked like a fool. I have shouted on nothing. I praised Him without a dime. I paid for it!

Let me give you these points. I feel something moving in me. I hear the Holy Ghost. I'm helping somebody in here. Put your hand on your neighbor's shoulder and say, "Don't be afraid to pay for it!" Don't be afraid to pay for it. Pay for it because the Lord has something good waiting for you. Slap another neighbor a five and say, "You are going to have the last laugh." Folks may be laughing now, but you will have the last laugh. It is like the last dance. My God! I will dance on you, over you, and through you.

The first thing Elijah had to do was prepare to endure. Look at anybody and say "Endurance." You cannot go any distance if you haven't made up your mind, "I will endure. I don't know what I will have to endure. I don't know how long I will have to endure it, but I am going to stay with it. I have come too far. I have put too much time into this thing." Now if you just got saved yesterday, you will understand it by and by. But if you have been saved for two weeks, you have put two weeks of time in. Do I have anybody here who has been saved 10 years? Anybody who has been saved 20 years? Anybody who has been saved 30 years? You have put too much time in it, honey. Don't let the devil back you up in the corner. You've got a right to come out, and you've got a right to go on. You better learn how to endure. Straighten your shoulders, throw your head up, hold your hands out and go on. Be steadfast, unmovable, always abounding in the work of the Lord. You know that your labor in the Lord is not in vain. Be not weary in well doing because if you hang in there and faint not, you shall reap a bountiful blessing. I was young and now I'm old, but I have never seen the righteous forsaken. Clap your hands and holler, "Yes!" You must prepare yourself to endure.

Secondly, the text says Elijah prayed and fell a sleep, and the angel cooked him some food. Can you imagine it? You open your eyes and there is an angel of the Lord cooking you some food. The text says the angel baked Elijah some bread and put a pitcher of water at his head and said, "Rise man, eat and drink." If you know anything about symbolism you know that bread is always represented as the Word of God, and the Holy Spirit is often represented in a liquid form of water. So what the angel told him was, "Get up and eat the Word and the Holy Ghost." I dare you to look at anybody and tell them, "The Word is in me and the Holy Ghost is over me. I can handle anything!" Say "Yes Lord!" Elijah fell asleep a second time -- it's in the text -- and a second time the angel cooked and brought him something to drink. The angel touched Elijah a second time and said, "Arise and eat. Arise and drink because you will need the strength of this Word and the strength of the Holy Spirit to take you 40 days."

The second requirement is you have to have some strength. You cannot endure anything without strength. Forty is the number of testing and trying and it is the number of victory. Let me qualify why the angel told Elijah 40 days. The Bible says in Genesis that when God was tired of man, He told Noah to build an ark and He tried and tested him for 40 days and nights. After 40 days and nights, Noah opened up the window and sent a dove out. The victory was in the ground because the ground was dry. The children of Israel marched in the wilderness for 40 years, but after 40 years, the Lord spoke to Joshua and told him to go on over and get the victory in the land. Moses sent spies into Canaan and they stayed in Jericho for 40 days. After 40 days and nights, they came back and told Moses the grapes are large and the pomegranates are sweet. In other words, the land is fruitful and God has kept His promise. Jesus was in the water, baptized by John. God spoke from heaven and said, "This is my beloved son in whom I am well pleased." The Bible says that when Jesus stepped out of the water, he was lead into the wilderness where he was tempted of the devil and without bread or water for 40 days and nights.

Elijah stood up on the mountain and the angel of the Lord told Elijah to eat a second time, eat the bread, eat the Word, and drink the water of the spirit because you are going to journey for 40 days. But after 40 days, I will give you the victory. You didn't read it, but let me tell you what the victory was. In verse number nine, the Bible says that Elijah jumped up on the strength of that meal and he wandered in the wilderness. He came to a cave in the mountain. When you look up the text in commentaries, the mountain that Elijah came to was named Sinai. If you know anything about Mt. Sinai, then you know that Sinai is the same mountain where God visited Moses. God's presence was at Sinai. I came to tell somebody that you've got to make it to the right place. That is your third requirement. If you are preparing to go the distance, you got to get to the right place.

When Elijah got to Sinai he went inside a cave, and

as he was in the cave the Lord God started talking to him. I wonder why God would talk to him in a cave. Why would God show up at such an unlikely place? Well, I'm glad you asked. God specializes in showing up at unlikely places. He showed up at a wedding when the wine was running low. He showed up at Simon, the leper's house, when he was dying from an incurable disease. He showed up at a cemetery where Lazarus had been buried for four days. Slap that neighbor on the shoulder and say, "You have to get to the right place." You have to prepare yourself to go the distance, so you can move in the right direction. You have to prepare yourself, so you can move in the direction of the blessing.

When Elijah came out of the wilderness and went to the cave, he went from a dry place to a holy place. I need somebody in Calvary to make up their mind, "I'm going to go the distance. I'm going to prepare myself for the journey because I have to make it to the holy place. I have to get myself online." Look at you neighbor and say, "Neighbor, I'm getting ready to go the distance because I'm getting ready to go online." You know what it means to go online? It is an Internet phrase and when you go online, you can search out the worldwide web. When you go online you can find out anything—like on AOL. Well, I have an acronym for AOL. AOL means I'm "anointed online." What that means is you may be ahead of me, but as long as I'm online I'm "AOL." You may be at the head of the line, but I'm "AOL." I'm anointed on the line up. Lean on your neighbor for the last time and say, "Neighbor, I may not look like I'm anointed and you may not think that I'm anointed, but I'm anointed on the line up. It's a good thing for you that you sat beside me because since you sat beside me, you are anointed on the line too."

I don't know what you believe God for, but if you can go the distance, He promised to open up the windows of heaven. He promised to meet all of your needs. He promised to give you the desires of your heart. He promised to order your steps. He promised no good thing will He withhold from them who walk online. He promised weeping may endure for a night, but joy will come in the morning. I'm prepared to go the distance. Whatever it takes, whatever I have to do, and wherever I have to go, I don't care. I'm prepared to go the distance. I'm yours, Lord! Everything I got . . . I'm yours, Lord. Try me, Lord, give me an experience. Try me and see if I can be completely yours.

This is an individual word. It is not a group thing today. Don't hold anybody's hand. You have to make it for yourself. If you want to know God, you have to know Him through your own experience. If you trust Him, you will trust Him because He has taught you something. Nobody can go this way for you. If you make it to this next level, you will have made it because you struggled through. You prepared your heart for endurance and you've made up your mind that you cannot go back. I will not go to the left. I will not go to the right. I refuse to step back. If I don't go forward, I will die where I am. I will endure. He that has begun a good work in me will perform it. Great is the presence of God in me. I'll get some strength some way during this experience of endurance. The Lord is going to bake me a cake. He will put something over my head and He will do it more than once. He is going to strengthen me and though the outward man perished, the inner man is renewed day, by day, by day. I will endure. I'll get strength from Zion. I'm going to move in the right direction. There is a prepared place where God wants to meet me. Elijah had to get to the cave because the presence of God was already there. Close you eyes and bow your heads.

Dear God, our father, we thank you today for speaking so candidly to our spirits. Sometimes when we feel so depleted, so worn, and so useless, just a word from You speaks to our hearts, encourages our spirits, lifts up our heads, and puts music in the air. You are a God who can do it. Take every experience and teach us something. It is impossible for us to know You aside from what we have experienced with You. If it means that we go to the wilderness and sit down under a tree, teach us there. If it means we have to walk to a mountain and declare your greatness, meet us there. We hide ourselves in a cave and a whirl wind goes by and says nothing. The floodwaters come and they speak nothing. But then there is a still small voice that says, "I will never leave you and never forsake you. I will take you where I want you to go and make you what I want you to be in spite of your circumstances. I am God in every situation."

Thank you for preparing us to go the distance. You would not bring us here if You didn't want to take us there. You would not take us there if You didn't want to take us all the way. Bless us individually today. Everything we've gone through, cause it to be a sound of the rain that shall come. Give us the abundance of a latter day harvest and if it means, dear Father, that we stay right here, that our hands are continually bruised and our eyes are still filled with tears . . . if it means that our hearts will still be broken and our minds yet confused . . . if it brings glory to You, then have your way and let it be so. There is a great reward when we do it your way. Bless us now. Make us a blessing. As we lift our hands in worship, we declare our bodies to be the temple of the Holy Ghost. Bread of heaven, feed us. Feed us until we want no more. Fill our cups, let them over flow. Fill them up Lord. We must go the distance. Send your anointing as we wait online. Send your anointing as we stand in your presence.